Creation

Creation

by

Johann Andreas Quenstedt

Theologia Didactico-Polemica
Part I, Chapter X
Third edition, 1696

edited, abridged, translated, and briefly
annotated
by
Luther Poellot

REPRISTINATION PRESS
MALONE, TEXAS

paperback edition published in 2019

REPRISTINATION PRESS
716 HCR 3424 E
MALONE, TEXAS 76660

E-mail: HUNNIUS@AOL.COM

ISBN 9781891469770

Table of Contents

Translator's Preface   vii

Abbreviations   ix

Section I: Didactic—20 Theses   1

Section II: Polemic

Question I—Does the creation of the world out of nothing, which occured in time, or with newness of being, stand in the light of nature, or is it an article of pure faith?   19

Question II—Did the world, or anything besides God, exist from eternity, or could it have been created from eternity?   29

Question III—Is there one creator of heaven and earth, Father, Son, and Holy Spirit, and are these Three Persons of the Godhead to be called associated causes of creation?   41

Question IV—Can the power to create be communicated to a creature?   51

Question V—Were all things created out of nothing in the beginning?   63

Question VI—Were all things made together and in one instant?   73

Question VII—Was a primitive and unarranged mass made in the beginning, which provided the matter of the heavenly and elementary bodies?   83

Question VIII—Are there waters above the firmament of heaven?   95

Question IX—Was the heaven that they call empyrean, which provides a palace for God and a dwelling place for God and a dwelling place for the angels and saints, created before all things?   107

There is no question that after the Loci Theologici *of Chemnitz and Gerhard (who was his uncle) the* [Theologia ... siva] Systema *of Quenstedt ranks as the greatest dogmatics book ever written by a Lutheran ... One might say that Quenstedt's* Systema *killed systematic theology in the period of Lutheran orthodoxy as Michelangelo killed Renaissance art by the unexcelled quality of his work.*
Robert Preus

Translator's Preface

Time takes its toll. At 86, this may be my last effort to give a 20th/21st-century voice to J. Quenstedt (1617–88; prof. Wittenberg; champion of orthodox Lutheranism). Previous publications in this series of chapters selected from his 48-chapter *Theologia ... siva Systema*: Part I, chaps. 1–3, *The Nature and Character of Theology*, Concordia Publishing House, St. Louis, Mo., 1986, Part IV, chap. 12, *The Holy Ministry*, Concordia Theological Seminary, Fort Wayne, Ind., 1991; Part IV, chap. 15, *The Church*, Repristination Press, Malone, Tex., 1999.

"Abridged" on the title page of these publications does not refer to the substance and content of the text itself, but only to documentation of authors quoted or referred to. Such documentation is one of printings most fruitful sources of errors in numbers and other matters, and it was not possible for me to verify and to make necessary or desirable corrections. The names of some obscure authors have also been omitted as serving no purpose in the present work.

"Edited" on the title page of these publications obviously refers not to the author's original manuscript, but to the third (1696) edition of his work. Inadvertencies (errors of various kinds) have been corrected. Perhaps some have not been caught. New ones may have crept in. But no part of the text itself has been edited out or changed substantively.

Later editions are not always better than earlier ones. For some of my work I had access to the 1715 edition, thanks to Concordia Seminary, St. Louis, Mo. But while the 1715 edition corrected some errors of earlier editions, it repeated some—and added some new ones. So which edition is the best? An unknown hand wrote in pencil, in German, on the title page of my copy of the 1696 edition: "*Beste Ausgabe*" [Best Edition].

For my readers, including the critics, I wish only the best of everything. Let them profit, so far as possible, from my work, correct and improve it as necessary or desirable, and complete Quenstedt's *Theologia* in English.

Need we follow Quenstedt in all that he says? No. Nor do we follow Luther in all that he wrote. "Prove all things; hold fast that which is good," 1 Thess. 5:21.

𝕬bbreviations

Genesis	Gen.	Zechariah	Zec.
Exodus	Exo.	Malachi	Mal.
Leviticus	Lev.		
Numbers	Num.	Matthew	Mat.
Deuteronomy	Deu.	Romans	Rom.
Joshua	Jos.	1 Corinthians	1 Cor.
Judges	Jud.	2 Corinthians	2 Cor.
1 Samuel	1 Sam.	Galatians	Gal.
2 Samuel	2 Sam.	Ephesians	Eph.
1 Kings	1 Kin.	Philippians	Phi.
2 Kings	2 Kin.	Colossians	Col.
1 Chronicles	1 Chr.	1 Thessalonians	1 The.
2 Chronicles	2 Chr.	2 Thessalonians	2 The.
Nehemiah	Neh.	1 Timothy	1 Tim.
Esther	Est.	2 Timothy	2 Tim.
Psalms	Psa.	Titus	Tit.
Proverbs	Pro.	Philemon	Phm.
Song of Solomon	SSo.	Hebrews	Heb.
Isaiah	Isa.	James	Jam.
Jeremiah	Jer.	1 Peter	1 Ptr.
Lamentations	Lam.	2 Peter	2 Ptr.
Ezekiel	Eze.	Revelation	Rev.
Daniel	Dan.		
Hosea	Hos.		
Obadiah	Oba.		
Jonah	Jon.		
Micah	Mic.		
Nahum	Nah.		
Habakkuk	Hab.		
Zephaniah	Zep.		
Haggai	Hag.		

Section I: Didactic

Thesis I

Some actions of God are inward,[1] some outward.[2] The inward actions of God are directed to the object that is God Himself, and they are either essential or personal. The inward essential actions of God are those that are limited[3] to God Himself and acknowledge, as the source of action, the divine essence, inasmuch[4] as it is common to all three Persons of the Godhead; e.g., an act of perception, by which God knows His very own self, and an act of the will, by which He acquiesces in Himself, as I were [in] the highest good. And these inward essential works are undivided, that is, they are common to all three Persons of the Godhead.

Thesis II

The divine inward personal actions are those that are limited to God Himself in such a way that they, on the other hand, do not acknowledge the divine essence as the source of action inasmuch as it is common to all three Persons, but as it is determined by certain personal characteristics and properties. Hence these inward personal works are divided, that is, they are not common to the three divine Persons, but belong to only one Person or to two Persons. And such works either [1] are from eternity, like the begetting of the Son and the spiration of the Holy Spirit, or [2] they take place in time, like the sending of the believers to perfect the work of sanctification. To beget and send the Son is [the act] of the Father alone; to spirate and send the Holy Spirit [is the work that] belongs to the Father and the Son.

Note: The inward works are not to be confused with the internal works. For although the internal works are immanent and eternal, yet they are not inward works, because they are not limited in the divine essence itself, but have regard to something that is outside of God; thus, e.g., to desire the salvation of mankind is an internal act of God and at the same time an outward act by reason of the object and end to which it tends, as will next be said.

Thesis III

The outward actions of God are those that are directed to an object that is not God Himself, but something other than God, or outside of God. And some [outward actions] are internal, or immanent, others [are] external, or emanent.

Thesis IV

The internal, or immanent outward actions of God are those that are indeed directed to an object located outside of God, yet are done, so to say, within the very bosom of the Godhead. Of this kind are both, the act or divine perception, by which God knows the ways of all people, as well as the act of the divine will, by which He wants their salvation. The object (e.g., the ways of people [and] the salvation of people), to which they are directed, or around which they internal actions of God, like perception and will, revolve is something other than God Himself and outside of God, and therefore also those actions are called outward. But because these actions of perception and go the divine will are performed and remain within the divine essence, therefore they are called internal and immanent actions. And these works are undivided, that is, common to all three Persons of the Godhead, yet with their order and difference intact.

Thesis V

External, or emanent and transient,[5] outward actions are and are called those that both [1] have regard to and object located outside of God (which they have in common with internal outward works) and [2] are performed outside of God and also produce or leave an effect located outside of God; and in this they are distinguished from the internal, or immanent, outward actions, and in turn they are either personal or essential.

Thesis VI

The personal outward actions are those that, performed outside of the bosom of the Godhead, belong to one certain Person by οἰκονομικὴν [administrative] appropriation.

Note: The personal outward actions are [1] in a certain respect and way, also essential, or common to all three Persons, namely by reason of the productive power, or principle, and inchoatively, but [2] personal or proper to one certain divine Person, by reason of the terminus, or terminatively, because they are terminated in a certain Person. Thus the Holy Spirit alone appeared in the form of a dove, Mat. 3:16. The voice from heaven, "This is My beloved Son," was [that] of the Person of the father alone, Mat. 3:17, and the Son of God alone appeared in the form and appearance of a man at the time of the Old Testament, and in the New Testament He was born of the Virgin Mary and [was] made flesh, Gal. 4:4; John 1:14; 1 Tim. 3:16. And yet also this flesh of the Son alone, and that voice of the Father alone, and that form of a dove of the Holy Spirit alone is a general work[6] of the Most Holy Trinity.

Thesis VII

Divine outward external essential actions are those that are concerned with some external object outside of the Godhead and are undivided, that is, equally common to all three Persons, yet with the orders and distinction of the Persons kept intact.

For although the action itself is essential, and the principle of acting [is] also one and the same, yet the manner and order of acting is different, for this distinct reason, that the three Persons have that principle or divine essence. For since the Other has the essence on His own,[7] therefore He also acts on His own. But the Son acts and works from the Father, and the Holy Spirit [works and acts] from the Father and the Son. The Father works through the Son and the Holy Spirit, but not the other way around.

Thesis VIII

Divine outward emanent actions are either [1] of power, like the creation and preservation of the world, or [2] of mercy, like the redemption, calling, regeneration, conversion, [and] salvation of mankind, or [3] or righteousness,[8] like the resurrection of the dead, the Last Judgment, [and] the damnation of the devils and the wicked.

Thesis IX

The prime work of divine power is the creation of this universe, which is nothing else than the external action of the triune God by which He brought forth all things visible and the invisible out of nothing, in six days' time, by the sole power of His completely free will, to the praise of His name and the benefit of mankind.

Note I: Creation is a work of God (1) single and perfectly simple by reason of its principle; (2) it is an act of the entire Most Holy Trinity, for it is an outward work; (3) it is an act of completely free divine will, (4) a direct act, which admits no creatures into joint action,[9] and finally, it is a most powerful, extremely wise, and excellent act.

Note II: The word "creation" is taken either improperly or properly. Taken improperly it denotes (I) The continued propagation and preservation of species, which is nothing else than continued creation, of continuation of creation. Psa. 104:30: "You will send forth Your Spirit, and they will be created."[10] Observe: By "Spirit" in

6

this passage some understand the energy by which living things live; but others, like blessed Gerhard, Geier, and the Belgians, explain it more correctly of the creating, life-giving, and renewing Holy Spirit. The Chaldean also takes it to mean "the Spirit of Your holiness." And the Psalmist doubtless had in mind the words in Gen. 1:2: "The Spirit of God moved over the waters,[11]" namely giving them seminal and prolific power and making them ready for the creation of living things. But the passage cited does not speak of creation of new species, but of other individuals by substitution in place of those that perished. Therefore the word "create: is used, because that perpetuity and propagation of species is, as it were, a kind of continual creation. Thus also Psa. 102:18: "The created people," that is, to be born, or still to be newly brought forth in the ordinary way of human generation, "will praise God." (II) Regeneration and renewal, which is, as it were, a kind of second creation, ἀνάκτισις καὶ ἀναπλασις [a rebuilding and a new formation]; Psa. 51:10: "Create in me a clean heart, O God, "that is, out of Your pure grace, without me cooperating in any way whatever, perform this singular work of recreation. Therefore the regenerate are called "a new creature," 2 For. 5:17; Gal. 6:15; Eph. 2:10. Now, the regeneration, conversion, and renewal of man is called creation in the Scriptures because it truly is no less a miracle than creation out of nothing. (III) The raining down of God's altogether righteous judgements. Isa. 45:7: "I, the Lord, form the light and create darkness, make peace and create evil." Now, God speaks of the evil of punishment or [of] calamities that He rains down. (IV) The bestowal of divine blessings, Isa. 41:20; 45:7; 57:19. (V) Finally, doing marvelous things. Thus the word "creation" is used of the stupendous miracle and the unheard of display of divine wrath, that the earth should devour Korah,

Dathan, and Abiram with an open mouth, as it were, Num. 16:30: "If the Lord create a new thing," that is, if He make something hitherto unseen; this also Jer. 31:22, where it is used of that altogether new and indescribably holy encircling,[12] by which the Virgin Mary embraced and conceived the Messiah in [her] sanctified womb. The prophet says: "The Lord created a new thing on earth."

Note III: The word "creation" taken properly denotes [1] primarily, or principally, the production of something out of purely negative nothing, how the primeval, original, formless universe[13] was brought into being out of nothing, that is, out of no preexistent or previously present material, Gen. 1:1; and [2] secondarily and less principally it means bringing something into being out of some material indeed previously present, but unfit and disordered, how, out of the original and unarranged mass, heaven and earth were made by God, how man was made out of a mass of earth, Gen. 1:27; 2:7, and woman out of a rib of the man, Gen. 2:21.

Thesis X

The efficient Author, of Cause of creation is the one and sole omnipotent and all-wise God, Father, Son, and Holy Spirit.

Note [1]: That God is the efficient Cause of creation is proved by the particular seat of this article, Gen. 1:1 ff., as well as by Jer. 32:17 [and] Acts 4:24. And that God alone is the Creation is proved (1) from Scripture, Job 9:8: "Who alone spreads out the heavens," and Isa. 44:24: "I, Jehovah, making all things, alone stretching forth the heavens, spreading abroad the earth by Myself." Hence Augustine says: "None but He Himself [God] made every incorporeal[14] creature." (2) From the clear thought: For creation, which is the production of a being out of nothing, from not existing to existing, infinite power and strength are required, Isa. 40:26; 42:5; as God alone possesses this [power and strength], so He alone also can create.

Note II: Now, that the Father, the Son, and the Holy Spirit created the world is proved (1) in general from the common theological rule: The outward works of God are undivided and [are] common to all three Persons, with the order and distinction of Persons intact. (2) From the unity of essence and power. For just as there is ἑνότης [unity], or oneness, of essence and power. For just as there is ὁμοιότης [likeness], or equality, in the manner of working and ταυτότης, or identity, in the work, yet with the distinction and order of the Persons intact, John 5:19; 1 Cor. 12:6 and 11. (3) From the account of creation, in which the work of creation, proper to God alone, (a) is attributed to more than one Person by the special term *Elohim* [God; a plural form in Hebrew] created, and the plural forms of expression: "Let us make man in our image." (b) Yet not to more than three Persons, who are both there and elsewhere in the Scriptures called either God in the absolute sense, or the Father, the Word or the Son, and the Holy Spirit, e.g., Psa. 33:6: "By the word of the Lord were the heavens made, and all the host of them by the breath[15] of His mouth." In particular is creation ascribed to (I) God the Father, 1 Cor. 8:6: "One God, the Father, from whom [are] all things"; Heb. 1:2: God has spoken to us very recently[16] by [His] Son, by whom also He made the worlds." Here observe: (1) God the Father is said to have made the worlds,[17] or the world,[18] by the Son, not as by an instrument, as the Arians rave, but by consubstantial wisdom and power, Pro 8:27; John 1:3; Col. 1:16. (2) By the turn of phrase there is indicated the order of personal acting; and it is false that the particle διὰ, "by," always points out the instrumental cause, because it is used also of God the Father, Rom. 6:4; 1 Cor. 1:9; Eph. 1:1. (II) Creation is ascribed to God the Son, Pro. 8:30, where Wisdom says: "I was אָמוֹן, a workman, by Him in the work of creation." Observe: In Pro. 8:22-30 the Son of God is extolled[19] by eternity, v. 30 by the work of creation, wisely carried out with God the Father; at the same time there is expressed both [1] distinct personality by its word אֶצְלוֹ at His side, and [2] the divine power in the skillful construction of the world; for אָמוֹן means a skillful workman; therefore blessed Luther rightly translated *"ein Werkmeister"* [master builder]. John 1:3: "All things were made by His (λόγον) [the Word]." Observe: (1) πάντα [all things], he says, al things absolutely and simply, not only the invisible things, as the Manichaeans of old fancied, nor only the things that pertain to the matter of salvation and religion in the time of the New Testament, as the Socinians would have it, but all things that are in heaven and on earth. For wherever in the New Testament the term τὰ πάντα [all things] is connected with words that mean either the first creation or preservation and governance, there it is altogether to be taken of all created things, Rom. 11:36; Phi. 3:21; Heb. 2:8 and 10. Observe: (2) The word ἐγένετο, "were made," does not mean an accidental change of human beings by which they become reborn out of nonreborn, as the Socinians hold, but it indicates the substantial production, or creation of all things. (3) The particle διὰ [by] is not the mark of an instrumental cause, but of a principal [cause]; hence it is used also of the Father; see the passages cited above. Col. 1:16: "By Him were all things created that [are] in heaven, and that [are] on earth, visible and invisible" etc. Observe: The Socianians object: "The point here is not the first, but the second creation, I.e., recreation and renovation." But wrongly. For (1) among the things that are said here [to be] created by Christ are listed also the angels, who, however, are not renewed by Christ [and] who have no chronic nature prone to sin. (2) All things are said to be created not only by Christ, but also εἰς αὐτὸν, "for Him," i.e., for His glory which belongs to God alone, Rom.11:36; 1 Cor. 8:6. The Socinians object further: "Scripture tells of the first creation by the production of heaven and earth, but not of the things contained [in] heaven and earth." We reply: (1) This statement is refuted by Isa. 45:7 and 66:2; Heb. 3:4. (2) Because there is nothing in this whole universe that cannot be reduced to those two kinds, visible and invisible, therefore the apostle adds, "All things were created by Him."

[Note] III: The work of creation is ascribed to the Holy Spirit, Gen. 1:2: "The Spirit of the Lord moved over the waters." Observe: (1) Some here understand air or wind by "Spirit." But nowhere is wind. Called "the Spirit of Elohim." In fact, the air did not exist until the second day, and so neither [did] rapid motion of the air, namely wind. All of the orthodox hold that here the Third Person of the Godhead is meant by "Spirit of the Lord, " for that [Person] is the Spirit of Elohim, I.e., of the Father and the Son, Mat. 10:20; Gal. 4:6. (2) The word מְרַחֶפֶת [moved] is expressive, for it mean that the Holy Spirit, like a hen brooding eggs, warming [them] and, as it were, giving [them] life, warmed the waters and gave life to bodies, so that, with the Father speaking, the Son creating and the Holy Spirit giving life, all creatures were made, as Arnobius says on Psa. 147. Job 33;4: "The Spirit of God has made me, and the breath of the Almighty Thunderer has given me life." Observe: By the thrust of the terminology, the Spirit of God and the breath of the Almighty is that Spirit and the breath, which is in God, or within God, which Enjedinus[20] himself cannot deny. Now, that the Spirit of God and the breath of the Almighty is not an attribute, but a Person of the Godhead is proved by the predicates. For to create and to give life is, in the proper sense, of Persons, and in this passage both are ascribed to the Spirit of God.

Thesis XI

There was no instrumental cause of creation; of such there is none in instantaneous action nor need of an preparation, nor could there be in the production of things out of nothing; for, you see, what does not exist cannot be prepared by an instrumental cause.

Thesis XII

Neither was there any προηγουμένη [antecedent] cause of creation, except the gracious purpose of God alone, communicating Himself, not from the necessity of nature, but from the freedom of [His] will.

Thesis XIII

There is no material of creation out of which[21] with regard to things created on the first day of creation. For they were created on the first day, not from preexistent material, either eternal or previously created, but were made out of purely negative nothing, this is clear (I) from the proper meaning of the word ברא, to create, which implies creation of something out of purely negative nothing. (II) From the circumstances of the text, Gen. 1. The context itself demands this creation[22] of heaven and earth out of nothing. For in the beginning, when creatures began to exist by creation, the Creator alone existed; with Him alone existing, all things, except for Him, were nothing. (III) From the sacred paraphrase of creation, which is this: "God calls τὰ μὴ ὄντα ὡς ὄντα, nonexisiting things as existing," Rom. 4:17; τὰ βλεπόμενα, the things that are seen, μὴ ἐκ φαινομένων, not of things that do appear, Heb. 11:3. And the things that were made on the other day were made out of material [that was] indeed previously present, but disordered (and not by any ordering power of secondary causes) and crude[23] (and in which is only the ability to obey, or the ability not to resist, in correspondence with the primary cause acting with infinite power:, namely out of the works of the first day, or out of that elementary and unarranged mass of heaven and earth, Gen. 1:1. Therefore all things were created out of nothing, some, however, directly, namely the works of the first day, the others indirectly, namely by means of the material that God had previously created out of purely negative nothing, namely the works of the following five days. Augustine rightly [says]: "God is for this reason altogether rightly believe to have made all things out of nothing, that although all things formed were made of that material, yet this material itself was made of absolutely nothing."

Note: where it is said that the works of the first day were created out of nothing, the particle *ex* [out of] does not designate material out of which, but excludes [it]. For by τὸ [the term] "out of nothing" nothing else is denoted than the starting point; that is, the nothing, from which all things are said [to have been] made, has respect not to the material, but only to the starting point[24], and ought to be understood of the order of creation, and the particle *ex* [out of] can be correctly translated by "after," so that the sense is, as Thomas[25] says: "After nothing, as the starting point, something was made."

Thesis XIV

The form of creation consists in external action, by which, partly our of nothing, partly out of material [that was] altogether crude and unfit, without motion or change, even [without] great effort, alone by the direction and command of [His] free will, by infinite power, all things were brought into being by God.

Note: The action of creation is completed in three steps: (I) The production, accomplished on the first day, of the original[26] material, which was the seedbed, as it were, of the whole universe. (II) The distinction and disposition of simple creatures, accomplished during the first three days. For, on the first day, [God] separated light from darkness; on the second [day], by an interposed firmament, [He separated] the waters beneath from those above; and on the third [day He separated] the earth from the waters. And (III) the furnishing and completion of the world, accomplished in the second three-day period. For, on the fourth day, [He] richly furnished the heavens with luminaries; on the fifth [day He richly furnished] the waters with fishes [and] the air with birds; [and] finally, on the sixth [day, He richly furnished] the earth with animals, and last of all, with the chief of all living beings, namely man.

Thesis XV

Therefore creation is divided into direct and indirect. The former is the creation of something out of nonexistence, or [out of] negative nothing. The latter is the forming out, or creation, of something out of clearly disordered material, which should be regarded as nothing, with regard to the thing to be created, by infinite divine power, without previous alteration. The former [the direct] is of the highest order and [is] creation, primarily, or principally so called, through which God, without the intervention of another, acted directly upon nothing, by calling forth from it that, which has a real and positive essence; but the latter is creation of the second order, secondarily and less principally, yet properly so called, by which God made something from material that indeed existed previously, but was crude and altogether disordered.

Thesis XVI

The ultimate end of creation is the glory of God. For in and through creation God manifested (1) the glory of [His] goodness, as He shared His goodness with creatures; (2) the glory of [His] power, as He created all things out of nothing, by [His] will and word alone; (3) the glory of [His] wisdom, which shines forth from the multitude, variety, order, harmony, etc. of created things. Psa. 19:1: "The heavens declare the glory of God."

Note I: By "heaven" in this passage, according to Basil the Great, Ambrose, and other interpreters, is meant the stupendous and supremely ingenious system of this visible heaven, the firmament, the sun and the rest of the stars, which we daily behold with our eyes. Now, the material heavens are said to delve the glory of God, not orally,[27] but by ingenious action,[28] or they present objectively the same as one presents who speaks distinct words. Or: they set before man praiseworthy material, so that he might acknowledge how good, wise, powerful, etc. God is. Pro. 26:4: "Jehovah has made all things *Lammaanehu*," which word is commonly translated "for His own purpose," so that the meaning is: God governs, ordains, [and] arranges all things, so that they correspond to His will, be it gracious or punitive.

Note II: The rhetorician Alcidamas speaks of the whole universe of things that strike our senses under an apt metaphor as τῆς φύσεως μουσεῖον, that is, a museum, as it were, of nature, in which all creatures, largest, middle-sized, [and] smallest, are set before our eyes and senses like common books, so that all the inhabitants of the world might read in them the goodness, wisdom, and power of God. The scholars say: "God does not act for the sake of His own benefit, but only out of His goodness."

Thesis XVII

The intermediate end [of creation] is the advantage[29] of human beings. For God made all things for the sake of man, but He made man for His own sake, Psa. 115:16: "The heavens, [even] the heavens [are] the Lord's; but He gave the earth to the children of men," that is to say: God resides in heaven; but He gave, for men to possess, the earth, enriched and endowed with the greatest variety of good things. Cf. Isa 45:18; Gen. 1:28.

Thesis XVIII

The effect of creation properly is a subsisting being, or substance. Accidents are created with substance, inasmuch as they have their being in them. Hereby we exclude ἁμαρτήματα [the defects] of nature, which began only after the Fall of man and are not so much effects as defects. The result, or end of creation is called visible and invisible creation, Col. 1:16.

Thesis XIX

Adjuncts of creation can be seen either [1] of creation considered formally or [2] of the same considered as to effect, or end, with regard to the created things themselves. In the former way, the adjuncts of creation are, that the action is supremely wise, supremely powerful, and supremely good, like the nature of its source, from which it issued, Rom. 1:20. In the latter way, the adjuncts of created things are [1] with regard to quality, [2] their goodness, [3] with regard to condition, their mutability, etc.

Thesis XX

Creation is neither the Creator not the creature, but it is in the middle between the creative power and the created thing. The reason is, that it is distinguished from both, also in regard to the matter; from the creative power,[30] for example, because this is eternal and intrinsically denotes the divine essence and is identified with the same. But creation, insofar as it means a transitive act, takes place in time and extrinsically denotes only its subject. And it is distinguished from created matter, as the act of going out directly from the divine essence, from a point outside of the divine essence, with the act of creation intervening, produced by creative power.

Note: Creation is not to be called a created thing; for [that] is called created, which is produced by creation; and so creation is the form, or reason why a created thing is called coated, but this external transient action of itself originates directly from God, without any other either or production; and yet it does not follow from this, that creation, on the part of the matter, is the divine essence itself, because it is not in God, but from God, and it works in time outside of the divine essence, and it denotes the subject, to which it is ascribed not intrinsically, but only extrinsically.

Notes:

1. *ad intra.*
2. *ad extra.*
3. *terminantur ad ipsum Deum.* The object of the action lies within the Godhead.
4. *quatenus.*
5. *transeuntes* in the sense of reaching out.
6. *universa operata.*
7. *a se.*
8. *justitiae.*
9. *in societatem.*
10. Quenstedt quotes the Vulgate Psa. 103:30: *emittes ... creabuntur.*
11. *super aquis.*
12. *circumdatio.*
13. *chaos.*
14. *quae non est.* Speculative translation.
15. *Spiritu.*
16. *novissime.*
17. *secula.*
18. *mundum.*
19. *commendur.*
20. A Socinian.
21. *materia ex qua.*
22. *effectionem.*
23. *inhabili.*
24. *terminus a quo.*
25. Thomas Aquinas.
26. *rudis.*
27. *vocis praeconio.*
28. *operis artificio.*
29. *utilitas.*
30. *a virtute ... creatrice.*

Section II: Polemic

Question I

Does the creation of the world out of nothing, which occurred in time, or with newness of being, stand in the light of nature, or is it an article of pure faith?

The Point at Issue

The question is not (I) about the Creator, but about creation itself; (II) not about creation in general, taken broadly and abstractly, but about creation in particular, taken in a narrow sense and formally; (III) not about a partial and imperfect knowledge of creation, but of total and perfect [knowledge]; (IV) not about the dependence of created things, but of the creation performed out of nothing, in time; (V) not about the power to create, but about the end of creating; (VI) not about the possibility of creation of the part of God, but about the possibility on the part of matter to be created, or created, namely whether this [creation] can be proved by natural reason. Briefly, the question is: Does the natural light of the human intellect know, or can it know, that creation took place out of nothing in time?

Thesis

The creation of the world, accomplished out of nothing in time, cannot be known from the light of nature or proved with absolutely certainty and clearly by philosophic lines of thought, but becomes known from sole divine revelation, and so it is an article of pure faith and revelation.

Exposition

I. One must distinguish between [A] creation taken γενικῶς [generically], or in general, broadly and in the abstract for the production of all things by God, in whatever or other way, time or order, finally, that was done, and in that way becomes known not only from Scripture, but also from nature, and [B] creation taken εἰδικῶς [in a special way], or in particular and in a narrow sense, and therefore in a formal sense for the kind of production of things that (1) took place out of nothing; (2) without previous change; (3) in the specific time and space of six days; (4) in the way and order prescribed by God; (5) by divine and incommunicable power etc. Since this is a matter of fact, it cannot be proved by a line of thought and therefore is also not to be sited among ἐπιστητὰ [matters of science], but among τὰ πιστὰ [matters of faith].

II. Observe: Blessed Meisner distinguishes between [1] total, or full and [2] partial, or imperfect knowledge. "Thus," he says, "one has some, or partial and imperfect knowledge of this article (indeed such perfection as one has here) is to be drawn from the Scriptures.

III. Some distinguish between [1] creation itself and [2] the manner and order of creation. They say that the former can be known by reason and the light of nature, but the latter by revelation alone.

IV. One must distinguish between [1] the efficiency and dependence of created things and [2] their creation out of nothing. That the world did not come into being by itself, but has [its] origin and dependence from another source, can be known also from the precept of reason. For if we run down the ladder of beings, we may consider the natures of the individual ones, [and] we see that, from the heaven to the world, the connection and harmony for mutual perfection is so great, that it could not but have been because it put together that series of beings and linked [it] together. Hence Augustine says: "Apart from the voices of the prophets, the world itself, silent in a way, proclaims by its altogether well-ordered mutability and mobility, as well as extremely beautiful appearance of all visible things, both [1] that it was created and [2] that only God could have created it." But, by reason of its form, creation itself does not become known except by supernatural revelation.

Antithesis

1. Of most of the scholastics, who do not doubt that the creation of things out of nothing can be

proved beyond all doubt by the light of nature and philosophic lines of thought; e.g. Thomas [Aquinas], [Henry] of Ghent; [Alexander] of Hales; [Duns] Scotus; also Suárez; they of Coimbra; etc.

Confirmation

That the creation of the world, made out of nothing, in time, can neither be known from the light of nature nor established by philosophic lines of thought we prove [I] from the statement of Scripture in Heb. 11:3: "By faith we understand that the worlds were framed by the Word of God," etc.

Note: (1) Whatever is known only by faith is neither known nor established by lines of thought. (2) Through τοὺς αἰῶνας [the worlds] this whole universe is understood just as [it is] now distinguished into its members, heaven, earth, sea, stars, stones, living things, [and] mankind. (3) The word κατηρτίσθαι [Heb. 11:3], which is "construct; form,[1]" expresses the order of formation and the procedure[2] of production by the Word of God, which become known not through nature, but alone through divine revelation. (4) One must observe here (a) knowledge, which is expressed by the word νοοῦμεν [understand (KJV)], for νοέω is "understand; notice," which is the first act of faith, embracing knowledge of things to be believed; (b) the object of the knowledge, which is creation, which is described, as to act, partly [1] by the word κατηρτίσθαι [form], by which both, the perfection of the work and its proper composing, is indicated, [2] partly by the words that follow, εἰς τὸ μὴ ἐκ φαινομένων τὰ βλεπόμενα γεγονέναι [so that the things (that are) seen were not made out of things (that were) visible], which speak of visible creatures by without excluding others, Col. 1:16. Τὰ μὴ φαινόμενα [the invisible things], that is, τὰ μὴ ὄντα [the things that are not] are the starting point. (3) The means is ῥῆμα θεοῦ [the Word of God], whereby the author, of principal cause, is also indicated. (4) The object of creation is indicated[3] by the word αἰῶνας, worlds, by which the apostle mean this whole universe. (5) The way of knowing is contained in the words πίστει νοοῦμεν [by faith we understand], which is not sensual, but mental knowledge, not science, but faith.

II. From the condition of creation, which, since it depends on the free will of God, and His determination is free from human intellect, cannot be searched out by human acumen. For nothing is certain regarding the free actions of God, except by revelation.

III. From the line of thought: Whatever is known,[4] is known either a priori [deductively] or a posterior [inductively]. The creation of things out of nothing can be [known] neither a priori [deductively] from nature, because it is a historical question, raised regarding a singular matter and fact, nor a posteriori [inductively], because, although the cause of an act can be know from the effect, yet at what time and in what way the cause produced it cannot be known, especially [a cause] freely causing the effect. Hence blessed Chemnitz rightly [says]: "Philosophy does not know creation out of nothing." With [his] whole chapter Chemnitz shows how imperfect and defective philosophy is in the doctrine of creation, and into what manner of opinions they fell, who wanted to draw the doctrine of creation out of philosophy.

IV. From the assertion of some scholastics: of [Gregory of] Rimini, Gabriel Biel, [and] Johann. de Bassoliis[5]; they hold that the light of reason cannot reach so far as to acknowledge that some kind of creation was made. The lines of thought run (1) from the ignorance of the best[6] philosophers who use the best natural light; (2) from the impossibility to demonstrate the origin of matter, [and] unless it is demonstrated, there is no demonstration of creation; (3) from the denial of the ways in which infinite power in the given act is demonstrated—yet, if it is not demonstrated, every attempt is frustration.

V. From either the defect of the weakness of the opposing lines of though; this becomes evident from the dissonant views of the philosophers themselves regarding the production of things.

Sources of Rebuttals

I. One must distinguish between [1] the efficient cause, of the Creator of the world, who is God and can be searched out, in a certain degree, by the light of nature, Rom. 1:20; for, you see, God "did not leave Himself ἀμάρτυρον, without witness," but gave witness through creation, Acts 14:27; and [2] its effect, of creation itself out of nothing, made in this order and way, which becomes known only by revelation.

II. Observe: The things that are found in the writings of the pagan philosophers or poets, regarding the creation of the world, are relics and remnants of patriarchal tradition, be they written or unwritten.

III. One must distinguish between [1] the power to create, which is by necessity of nature and can also be searched out by natural ways, and [2] the act of creating, which depends on the completely free divine will; as this is hidden to nature, so [is] also its completely free act. God called the creatures, so that they might be, when they were not—not by necessity of nature, but by the freedom of [His] will.

IV. One must distinguish between [1] possibility on the part of God, whether God can produce something out of nothing, and [2] possibility on the part of a thing to be created, namely whether something can be created out of nothing and at some time be made. Perhaps a philosopher will not deny the former as such, but in the latter, he will repeat the αὐτόπιστον [in itself credible] and ἀξιόπιστον [trustworthy] principle: Nothing comes out of nothing.

V. Observe: It is one thing for creation to be possible in this way, that it can come into being from a first cause, which is also indicated by nature, and [it is another thing] for creation to be made by an act, and that at certain time; the latter is unknown to nature.

VI. One must distinguish between [1] the knowledge of the pagans regarding the origin of the world, drawn from nature and the principles of reason, and [2] the knowledge gather from the reading of the Holy Scriptures, or [from] rumor, or [from] discussions with Jew or Christians; we grant the latter [and] deny the former. Indeed, the most ancient of the philosophers often say that the world was produced by some author and founder. But [1] it is not clear whether they say that as they follow human reason. [2] They speak not so much of true creation as of formation out of previously present matter. They also do not speak in an all-all-conclusive way of both [a] the visible, or sensible world and [b] the invisible, or intellectual [world]. For it can scarcely be perceived what they could not draw out of chaos.

VII. Observe: Although creation out of nothing does not conflict with reason, if it is rightly set forth with regard to an act of a a divine age, whose infinite power and might also a pagan philosopher cannot deny, yet creation cannot therefore also be known from reason. For it is one thing, not to conflict with reason, [and it is] another thing, to be known from reason. And it does not immediately follow, that what does not conflict with reason is also known from it [reason]. For that God acts in an infinite and marvelous way does not conflict with reason, and yet it is not clear from reason what, if you please, it is, that God does in an infinite and marvelous way.

VIII. (1) That it was possible for the world to have a beginning, (2) that all things have their beginning from the one and eternal God, [and] (3) that He communicates Himself to creatures by an act [that is] not natural or necessary, but free—these things can be shown from nature, but that the world began by an act, or was created at the beginning of time out of nothing is not evident and demonstrable in that way, unless one first has faith.

Notes:

1. Reading *apto* instead of *adapto*.

2. *rationem.*
3. Reading *indicatur* instead of *indicat.*
4. i.e., by the mind on its own.
5. I have no further information on him.
6. *accuratissimorum.*

Question II

Did the world, or anything besides God, exist from eternity, or could it have been created from eternity?

Thesis

The world neither existed from eternity, nor could it have been created from eternity.

Exposition

I. Observe: With regard to the question, whether the world could have been created from eternity, or in some imaginary moment of eternal duration, at least with regard to its primary material, Athanasius rightly replies: "Although it was possible for God to perform works from eternity, yet the things that were made could not have existed from eternity; now, since the things that were not, before they were, came forth out of nonentities and were not before they came into being, how could they have coexisted with God, who always existed?[1]"

II. Observe: That question (whether the world could have been created from eternity) does not concern the article of faith, and therefore neither view is to be accused of any heresy, much less atheism. For [1] neither do those, who deny that it [the world] could have been created from eternity, disparage infinite power, since they deny it not because of a defect of power in God, but because of the impossible object, because they hold that it involves a contradiction; [2] nor do those, who affirm, admit an actual eternal creation, but they only make it [eternal creation] possible, and they do not believe that [this] involves a contradiction.

Antithesis

I. Of most pagan philosophers, chief of whom was Aristotle, who hold that this visible world, or at least matter, existed ἄτομον [without interruption] from eternity. [Peter] Fonseca[2] indeed, and they of Coimbra, as well as Cornelius Martini[3] try to prove from Aristotle himself, that he acknowledged creation, but that which is without newness of being (creation without newness of being they call simple emanation of a thing from God, so that by nature that thing is indeed after[4] God, but not on a time line,[5] and so eternal creation and creation without newness of being are the same to the scholastics). But creation with newness of being is to them the kind of action by which a thing is after God not only by nature, but also on a time line, and in that way creation with newness of being is a new creation and accomplished in time. But that [1] creation, that is, the production of something out of nothing, and [2] the almighty power of God was neither recognized by Aristotle, nor does it agree with his principles, even long ago Eudemus and Alexander, noted peripatetics, said, according to Simplicius,[6] and most of the moderns,[7] like Peter Hurtado de Mendoza, affirm, saying: "What Aristotle and the preceding early age of philosophizers said, 'Nothing comes from nothing,' others set forth regarding natural agents. I hold that they did not recognize the almighty power of God." And Francisco Suárez says regarding Aristotle: "Wether he comprehended the omnipotence of God is not clear to me." Wilhelm Estius agrees with these. Sainted[8] [Johannes] Affelmann says: "Aristotle wants the problem to be a dialectical teaching regarding the eternity of the world, but he concludes; the brothers from Spain go about in vain to absolve him." Gassend says: "All philosophers" (he is speaking of heathen [philosophers]) "agreed to this, that material preexisted, out of which the world was made, because nothing is made out of nothing." Some attribute to Plato that God made the matter of the world, [which matter is] moving around, back and forth for infinite ages, before [He] brought it back into order out of that formless confusion. Basil the great conjectures that the reason for this error is drawn from the words in Gen. 1:2. Plato accordingly would have the world made, but out of eternal material—and that before infinite myriads of years. Proculus and Averroes follow Plato. Now, since the philosophers acknowledge that the noblest bodies are made anew, but out of previously present material that knows no beginning, why did they not fully apply the light of nature and observe that it is absurd to attribute a beginning to the noblest beings, but to equate matter with God in respect eternity? Or is it not better to say that both matter and all things in it and of it came forth out of the profundity of divine power?

II. Of the ancient heretics, who papered over the error regarding eternal matter; e.g., Marcion and especially Hermogenes the African, about whom Tertullian says: "Turned away from Christians to the philosophers, from the church to the Academy and the Porch, he learned from the Stoics [how] to put matter [on the same level] with the Lord, [as if] it and itself had always existed, neither born nor made, nor having any beginning or end at all, out of which the Lord afterward created all things." Tertullian himself also calls those heretics Materialists,[9] who regard some matter coeternal with God. From that Hermogenes, Daneau would have those called Hermogenians, also Hermians, whom Augustine notes to have said that the matter of the elements, of which the world was made, was not made by God, but [is] coeternal with God. The Seleucians,[10] as also the Procleanites, followed the error of the Hermians. And about the year 1270 some heretics in Paris taught, among other things, that the world is coeternal with God; they were condemned by Stephen, bishop of Paris.

III. The following inline toward the same heresy of the Materialists; (1) The Socinians, inasmuch as they deny that God made all things and regard matter [as] coeternal with God. Thus Smalcius and Moskorzowski, who says: "Those who have thoroughly looked into the writings of ancients and moderns on the same matter will admit that they, who want the prime matter [to be] eternal, do not rely on trivial reasons or on a weak foundation, which the Holy Scriptures may anywhere oppose." (2) The Arminians, for Episcopius held that it is nowhere said in [so many] words or without controversy, that matter was made out of nothing. (3) The response of Vorstius, who denies[11] that it is clear from the Scriptures that God did not create all these things out of some previously present material; he also denies that it is necessary to believe in creation out of nothing.

IV. [The Antitheses] of the founder of the pre-adamites,[12] who clearly tries to defend the eternity of the world deductively,[13] although he puts it [the eternity of the world] a step below diving [eternity].

V. Of the crassest naturalists, materialists, and speculative atheists, in Gaul, who deny all existence of a divine being and rave that matter existed ἄτομον [without interruption] from eternity, from the fortuitous[14] concurrence of which this whole universe is put together, and so they recognize no infinite Being distinct from natured nature.[15] Benedict [Baruch] Spinoza clearly indicated that by the name of God he understands nature, i.e., that this universe, existing of itself and by itself and not acknowledging any outward cause for itself, also admits absolutely no God besides nature or mundane, immeasurable, αὐτόζωον [self-existent] matter; Maresius therefore calls him an ex-Jewish[16] blasphemer and a formal atheist.

VI. Of most scholastics and papists, who hold

that the world could have been, and been made from eternity, not indeed as to all orders of creatures, but only as to those things that have some fixed and permanent, not successive, being, or whose essence does not lie in successions of motion or generation. Thus Gregory of Valencia and they of Coimbra. Others [hold it] only as to spiritual and incorruptible creatures, and not as to material and corruptible, but permanent things, like Thomas [Aquinas] and Gabriel Biel. Others [hold it] as to both permanent and successive creatures, except generations of substances and accidents; among these is Gabriel Vásquez. Others, finally, [hold it] also as to generations and corruptions of lesser things. Scotus, with his [followers], holds that both views are probable, namely that the world could have been made from eternity and that it could not have been so made. Hence Gilbert Voet says; "The scholastics and the more recent papistic theologians, as well as nearly all the philosophers, say that the world or some creation can be eternal; among them you may hear it said; 'Newness of being is not regarding the nature of a creature,' except for Scotus, who speaks problematically, and Marsilius [and others], who deny [it]."

Confirmation

I. That the world is not eternal, but was created in times, is proved (1) from the account of creation in Gen. 1, which Moses drew neither from the light of nature nor from tradition, inasmuch as [it (tradition) was] obliterated in large part by so great an interval of time, but solely from the special revelation of God.

(2) From the end and destruction of the world, foretold in the Scriptures. What ceases to be at a certain time also began to be at a certain time. Or, what is subject to destruction is not without beginning, not from eternity. Now, the world is subject to destruction, Mat. 5:18; 24:35; 1 Cor. 7:31; 2 Pet. 3:10; 1 John 2:17. Ergo.

(3) From eternity, [which is] proper only to God. If only God is eternal, neither the world nor any thing outside of God is or can be from eternity. Now, the former [is] true, Gen. 21:33; Isa. 40:28; 48:16; Rom. 16:26. Ergo. That something which is finite is coeternal with the infinite God conflicts also with sound reason, and for two infinities to be given [is] incongruous.

(4) From the manner of production. Since all things were created out of nothing, it follows from this, that the matter out of which [they were created] was not from eternity. "God said, 'Let there be light,'" Gen. 1:3, and by this word of God light, which previously was not immediately began to exist. God calls τὰ μὴ ὄντα ὡς ὄντα [the things that are not as though they were], Rom. 4:17. Therefore all things τὰ ὄντα [that are] were previously μὴ ὄντα [nonexistent.] The apostle clearly [says], Heb. 11:3: "By faith we understand that the worlds were formed by the word of God, εἰς τὸ μὴ ἐκ φαινομένων τὰ βλεπομένα γεγονέναι, so that visible things were made out of invisible things; τὰ [the] non-apparent things are nonexistent

things,[17] as Luther puts it, or τὰ μὴ ὄντα [things that are not], as the apostle says, Rom. 4:17. Voet [says]: "In short, creation is the production of something from nonbeing to being; one must therefore grant something present, not only of nature, but also of time, when it will not have been produced; from this it follows that it was not from eternity."

II. That the world could not have existed or been created from eternity is proved

(1) Because to be from eternity belongs to the one and only God, as said, so that whatever is eternal must be God. See the passages cited above [under] no. 3.

(2) Because it involves conflict as well [1] on the part of the creating God, because God, because God cannot produce another God different from Himself, [2] as on the part of the creature, which is not capable of existence from eternity. What cannot be, except after not being, cannot be from eternity. Now, no creature can be, except after not being; for to be created is to be produced out of nothing. What exists from eternity, exists without a beginning of its own; but whenever a creature is created, its very self comes into being, because every effect, inasmuch as it is produced by its own cause, comes into being and takes its being from the same cause; now, when a creature comes into being, its begins to be, and same cause; now when a creature comes into being, it begins to be, and if it begins to be, it could not exist from eternity. For [these] are contradictory; to exist with its own beginning, and not to exist with its own beginning.

(3) We know that the world was made in time; therefore we reject as curious and useless the question whether it could have been from eternity and hold it unworthy of the reply of Christians, since it is not revealed.

(4) Some add the argument from incongruity, because in that way the argument derived from eternity for the divinity of Christ would be rendered invalid. But blessed Doctor Calov replies. Just as the line of thought does not run like this: "Holy Scriptures say that the world was created in time; therefore it could not have been created in eternity," so the argument of the deity of Christ is not invalidated, which the Catholics strongly emphasize against the Arians; that the Son of God is eternal, because He existed in the beginning of creation and before all created things, if a possible eternal creation be established. So also holds Voet, because be it as it may regarding that possibility, it is certain from Scripture that there was nothing at the beginning of creation, when God began to create things, and [nothing] before creatures, except only the immeasurable God. Therefore the line of thought remains unshaken, that the Son of God, who was then already in the beginning, is Himself the immeasurable God.

(5) Zacharias of Mitylene says: "The world is not coeternal with God, since the things that are coeternal are at the same time,[18] and the things that are at the same time cannot mutually of themselves have an efficient cause."

Sources of Rebuttals

I. They object: There is no conflict if eternal creation is established [1] on the part of the creating God, because the power of God to create is not less than that of the sun to shine; but if the sun were from eternity, it would have shone from eternity. [2] Not on the part of the thing that is produced, because something in the world is from eternity, namely the Divine Word. Therefore [this is] no contradiction, that something is produced or receives [its] being from eternity. [3] Finally, not on the part of creation itself, because the term "out of nothing," in the definition of creation, is not taken in a positive sense, as though it denotes the order of the term under which the thing was previously, but in a negative sense, so that it is the same as not from another. We reply: (1) The examples of the power of the sun to shine and of the eternal generation of the Son are [in nature] different[19] [from creation]. For the sun could not even exist without shining, or God the Father without generation of the Son, but God can certainly exist without creation. God does not create because of necessity of nature, like illumination belongs to the sun and generation to God out of necessity of nature. God freely produces something different from His own essence and nature. (2) Since matter is said to be produced out of nothing by creation, not only is previously present matter denied, but the point is also noted, under which it was before production, namely τὸ [the] nothing.

II. They reply: If a foot had stood from eternity in dust, no one would doubt that under that foot there would have been from eternity a vestige that [was] made by the one stepping down. We reply: Again, the example does not fit. For creatures do not also necessarily exist in the same way, since God exists, as a vestige is necessarily imprinted on the dust in which a food steps down, because God called those things as though they were, when they were not, not by necessity of nature, but by freedom of the will. It happens naturally, if the foot of one who steps down imprints a vestige in the dust, just as a shadow naturally clings to a body; but that did not happen naturally when God created the world.

III. It is ἀκυρολογία [incorrect phraseology] to say that at one time the world was not. For τὸ [the word] *aliquando* [at one time] is the same as *aliquo tempore* [at a certain time], but it cannot be said that at a certain time the world was not, because there was no time before the world was established. One who says that the world was not always speaks more carefully.

IV. We do not say correctly that the world was creatable before it was created, or that it was within the ability for creation[20]; but we well say that it was possible, that the world be created. For since passive power does not exist, except in some subject who calls the world creatable, [it] posits passive power without a subject.

40

Notes:

1. *semper existente.*
2. A Portuguese Jesuit.
3. Prof. Helmsted; introd. Aristotelian metaphysics into Lutheran thought.
4. *posterior.*
5. *duratione.*
6. Greek Neoplatonic philosopher.
7. From Quenstedt's viewpoint.
8. *D.*; read here for *divus* in the sense of sainted, or blessed.
9. *Materiarios.*
10. Hermians associated with Seleucia.
11. Reading *negat* instead of *negant.*
12. That is, the originator of the theory: Isaac de la Peyrère (1594–1676; Bordeaux Huguenot); he later renounced the theory and became Roman Catholic ca. 1657.
13. a priori.
14. Reading *fortuito* instead of *fortitudo.*
15. *natura naturata.*
16. He was born of Port.-Jewish parents.
17. *aus nichts.*
18. *simul.*
19. *aliena.*
20. *in potentia ad creationem.*

Question III

Is there one creator of heaven and earth, Father, Son, and Holy Spirit, and are these three Persons of the Godhead to be called associate causes of creation?

Thesis

There is one creator of heaven and earth, Father, Son, and Holy Spirit, and these three Persons of the Godhead are not rightly called associate causes of creation.

Antithesis

I. Of the Simonioans, Gnostics, Menandrians, Corinthians, and the followers of Aconcio,[1] who say that the world was made not by God, but by the angels, as a work unworthy of God; also Saturninus, who said that the world was made by seven angels, without the consent of God the Father.

II. Of the Manichaeans, Marcionites, [and] Cerdonians, who hold two usually opposed principles, one good, the other evil, and rave that these are the cause of the world. Of the followers of Apelles and the Priscillianists, who said that there is one principle, a good God, and that another was made by Him, who [the other one], since he was evil, made the world in his malignity.

III. Of the Arians, who say blasphemously that the Father, holding to the work of creation unworthy of His majesty, entrusted it to the Son as lesser and inferior, and that He [the Son] commended some things in creation to the Holy Spirit, as to a helper, to be done; of them in particular the Dulian[2] offspring of the Arians called the Son of a servant and instrument of the Father and thus held that the world was made by Christ as an instrument of the Father.

IV. Of the Socinians, who deny that the Son of God is the creator of the world and hold that He is not the primary, but only the secondary cause of created things.

V. Of those who maintain that on the first day of creation the Spirit, or soul of the world was made to be a kind of future maker of the five days of the rest of creation.

VI. Of the Weigelians, who fancy that only the Father created man, and that man was created by God and [out of] nothing. *"Der Mensch war geschaffen von Gott und von nichts,"* says Weigel.

VII. Of the Calvinists, who call the three Persons of the Godhead associate causes of creation; e.g., Keckermann, who dreams up three who justify and three authors of justification, named the Father, the Son and the Holy Spirit; Polanus, who calls the Son an associate of the Father in creation; Bucanus, who calls God the cause of faith and [calls] the Son and the Holy Spirit συναίτια [coworkers] [and says]: "Κύριον αἴτιον [the main cause] for repentance itself is God, and the Holy Spirit [is] only a coworker"; Piscator, who thinks he sees three principal associate causes of salvation; Chamier, who envisioned a primary,[3] secondary,[4] and tertiary[5] cause of creation.

Confirmation

That there is only one creator of heaven and earth, Father, Son, and Holy Spirit, we have showed [to be] true[6] [in] section I, thesis X. For creation is a proper work of God alone. Athanasius expressed this aptly: "Administration is for creatures and servants; but to make and create is for God alone and His Word and Essence.[7]"

Now, that the three Persons of the Godhead are not associate causes of creation is proved by this, that in associate causes there is (a) diversity of causality, and where [there is] a diverse causality, there [are] diverse causes, diverse entities; (b) partiality and particularity of influence[8]; from this arises limitation and a division of works, neither of which is admissible[9] in the Godhead.

II. [Gregory of] Nazianzus says: "What acts is one Godhead common to three Persons"; therefore, just as [there is] one divine Essence and one power, so also is there one creative power, one act of creating, equally common to these very Persons, and therefore, only one creator. Now, where [there is] only a single creator, there distinct causes of creation cannot be set in place.

III. Distinct authors or distinct causes do not act in outward operations, but the cause is one, the author single, because the outward operations are undivided.

IV. Crocius rightly perceives that those have spoken ἀκύρως [improperly], who speak of three authors of creation and justification, and that it is more correctly said that the three Persons of the Godhead are one author of creation and justification, than three authors.

Refutation of Objections

I. Observe: When the apostle says, Rom. 11:36, "ἐξ αὐτοῦ, δι᾽ αὐτοῦ, καὶ εἰς αὐτὸν τὰ πάντα [of Him, through Him, and to Him (are) all things], there, according to the holy fathers, the little word ἐξ [of] is connected with God the Father, the little word διὰ [through] with God the Son, and the little word εἰς [to] with the Holy Spirit, yet these little words introduce no inequality of Persons of the Godhead in the work of creation, but only indicate their order. Gregory of Nazianzus rightly says that these little words, ἀπὸ, ἐν, δὶα [from, in, through], do not divide the nature of imply inequality of the divine Persons, but only express the properties of the one and unconfused nature.

II. One must distinguish between [1] a popular and less accurate way of speaking, in which the ancient fathers called God the Father the προταρκτικὴν [immediate exciting], the Son the δημιουργικὴν [formative], and the Holy Spirit the τελειωτικὴν [perfective] cause of creation; likewise that the Son of God served the Father and was His instrument in creation, etc. By this they only wanted to speak of a different kind of attribution and order of working. And [2] accurate terminology. Such ἀκυρολογίαι [incorrect phraseologies] of some fathers do not owe [their] being to deception on the part of well-known orthodoxy.[10]

III. One must distinguish between that little word διὰ, through, taken [1] in the instrumental sense and [2] taken in the architectonic sense. John the evangelist and the Nicene fathers take the little word διὰ, through, not in the former but in the latter way when they say that all things were made through the Son. In this way it is also usually used elsewhere of principal causes; hence it is used also of God the Father, 1 Cor. 1:9; Eph. 1:1; Rom. 6:4; Heb. 2:10. The Father created all things through the Son, not as through an instrument, but as through His [the Father's] ὑποστατικήν [personal] wisdom and power, Pro. 8:30. Not to say that an instrument is used to prepare matter, but there is no matter in the production of something out of nothing. Therefore also an instrument, and so the little word "through" is not a mark of a secondary and organic cause, but of the order of the divine Persons and of the distinct manner of working.

IV. Observe: Blessed Luther, in [his] exposition of Gen. 1, and likewise Heerbrand, call the Son of God an instrument of the Father in creation. But in that way, (1) Luther speaks in conversational writing, not in precise statement; (2) it is clear that both religiously defended the ὁμοουσίαν [consubstantiality] of the Father and the Son; therefore, with this turn of phrase, they wanted to indicate only the order of acting, and not some subjection or inferiority.

V. One must distinguish between [1] a separate instrument, such as a hammer and a rapier, and [2] a conjunct, or essential, or integral instrument, in figurative speech, in which way one's food and hand are instruments, as also the Holy Spirit in called the finger or God, who [the Holy Spirit] does therefore not cease to be the principal cause. Luther and Heerbrand meant the word "instrument" in the latter, not the former way; however, this way of speaking is to be condoned, rather than imitated.

VI. Observe: In the Apostles' Creed the work of creation is ascribed in particular to the Father (1) not exclusively, but inclusively, for the Son and the Holy Spirit are that same creator, (2) because of the singular manner and order of operation; for the Father acts of Himself, and the Son and the Holy Spirit [act] of the Father, (3) because power is ascribed to the Father, which [power] shines very brightly in creation, [and] (4) because creation, as the first work, is to be sacred to the First Person of the Most Holy Trinity, who manifested Himself in it in a special way. No preeminence, no disparity, also no partiality or causal fellowship are to be imagined here, but the Father, Son, and Holy Spirit are one principal cause.

VII. One must distinguish between [1] simple

action, in which a way of combining helpers and especially agents, likewise of works and endeavors and of labors, also by the same view, of powerful causes, is excluded; such action has a place in the Godhead; and [2] composite, mixed, human actions, where all those things are present.

VIII. One must distinguish between [1] a solitary cause [that is] sufficient by itself for producing an effect, [and] such a cause is God, and [2] an associated cause, which is only partly sufficient, and that is not the case here.

IX. One must distinguish between [1] coordinate causes, which are of the same kind, and [2] subordinate causes, of which one is the principal, the other instrumental; in the Godhead there is no subordination.

X. Observe: The Calvinists object: "Blessed Dieterich also envisioned three associated causes of creation." We reply: One does not find in Dieterich that he wrote that the three Persons of the Godhead are three associated causes of creation. He says this: "The causes are equal that work with equal power or that are of equal efficacy in association. Thus the power and might of the Father, the Son, and the Holy Spirit is equal in making the world." So we see that Dieterich says this, not to point out three associated causes of creation, but only to show equality in effective action.

XI. Observe: The cause, by whose power a thing is, is one thing, the order and mode of acting [is] another. One who calls God the Father the cause, and [calls] the Son and the Holy Spirit συναίτια [joint causes], he is seen to intimate a difference and to put the Son and the Holy Spirit below the Father as ministering causes, distinct from the principal cause; ὁμοουσία [consubstantiality] does not allow this.

XII. Observe: Coefficiency is one thing, and connection of associated causes [is] another. For they differ, as broader and narrower. Every associated cause is coefficient, but not the other way around, every coefficient cause is thereby associated. And so Crocius, defending Goclenius, less accurately tries to explain associated causes as coefficient and joined together. Moreover, we deny that the Father, the Son, and the Holy Spirit are coefficient, or conjoined causes of creation. [There is] no coefficiency here, where [there is] completely simple essence, one power, [and] one influence of causing, and so one efficiency. Nor is there any need of conjunction of causality where there is only one completely simply causality, since conjunction involves union and union is found only among more [than one].

XIII. Observe: Christ indeed says, John 5:17: "My Father works until now, and I work." But the Son also works, not with another different, but also with the same associated faculty of working, with which power the Father works. No mention is made here of confederate efficiency, no συνεργείας [joint work], but that ἐργάζεσθαι [working] of the Father is repeated with the same word in the same sense regarding the Son.

Notes:

1. *Achonticorum.*
2. *Duliani.*
3. *primam.*
4. *secundam.*
5. *tertiam.*
6. *probatum.*
7. *Substantiae.*
8. *influxus.*
9. *admittendum.*
10. *Orthodoxiae notariae fraudi esse non debent.*

Question IV

Can the power to create be communicated to a creature?

The Point at Issue

The question is not (I) about actual creation, for none of the Christians holds this view, but about communication of creative power; or, the question is not whether any creature ever produced of created some creature out of nothing, but whether any creature has or can have power to create. (II) The question is not whether God made any creature having power to create, but whether any creature can be made that is able to do this. "For God," as Mendoza says, "can create a thousand kinds of things other than those actually made." (III) The question is not about a creature as such that exists outside the Person λόγου [of the Word], but about a creature as such that exists outside the Person λογου [of the Word], or one that also has created subsistence. (IV) Not about creation spoken of improperly and metaphorically, but properly.

Thesis

Creation is a work of God alone in such a way, that the power to create or produce out of nothing can be communicated in any way to no creature that is outside λόγου ὑπόστασιν [the Person of the Word] either as to a principal cause or as to an instrumental [cause] of acting dependently or independently.

Exposition

I. One must distinguish between [1] αὐθυπόστατον [a self-substantial] creature, per se and existing outside λόγου ὑπόστασιν [the Person of the Word], and [2] a creature ὑπόστασαν [made Personal], or assumed into the divine Person, or existing within λόγου ὑπόστασιν [the Person of the Word], namely the human nature of Christ. The question is not about the latter, but the former. For since omnipotence is communicated to the human nature of Christ by virtue of the personal union, there is no doubt that also the power to create belonged to Him. But here we are speaking about created nature subsisting in its own personality.

II. One must distinguish between [1] communication by μετέκβασιν [outcome], into another subject, and [2] communication κατὰ συνδύασιν [by coupling], where ὑφιστάμενον [the basis] is one, with the divine and the created nature constant. That the infinite power to create was communicated to the flesh of Christ κατὰ συνδύασιν [by coupling] and by virtue of the personal union is certain from the Scriptures; by this infinite creative power He also made wine out of water, John 2. But with the basis divided by digressive communication, the creative power can in no way be communicated.

III. One must distinguish between [1] the word "creation" taken properly, and in that way it means production out of nothing, or as it were nothing, (or out of completely disordered matter, which is regarded as nothing with regard to producing something), Gen. 1:11 [and] 27; 2:3; Due. 4:32; Psa. 104:30; Isa. 42:5, and [2] creation taken improperly and metaphorically, and hence used of miracles, Exo. 34:10; Num. 16:30, Isa. 54:16, Jer. 31:22, of marvelous works of divine providence, Isa. 45:7 and 57:16, of the work of the renewal of a man, which is, as it were, a second creation, Spa. 51:10, and of the establishment of the church, Psa. 102:18; Isa. 43:1 and 15; 45:18. To creation improperly so called, that is, to the production of miracles and of other divine works, a creature can be applied as an instrumental cause, but not to creation properly so called, since there is nothing here, in which the work of a created instrument can be used.

IV. Observe: It is one thing to ask whether any creature actually created, and another [to ask] whether, by the absolute power of God, the creative power can be communicated from God to a creature. Most scholastics deny the former; that latter is affirmed by [Peter] the Lombard and Durand, whom [Durand] Roderic de Arriaga [a Jesuit] followed.

V. Observe: [1] It is one thing, whether the power to created can be communicated to a creature by the absolute power of God, as to an instrumental agent, or whether it can be assumed, as an instrument of creation, and [2] [it is] another, whether creative power can be communicated to the same, as to a principal care of dependent or independent action. We deny both in the Thesis. For there is a twofold question here. The one [is], whether there is or can be a creature that, as a principal cause, has in itself the power to created and produce something out of nothing; the other [is], whether a creature if it cannot create by native power and as a principal cause, can at least be assumed as an instrument of creation, and in that way there is no reason why God cannot use one creature as a instrument to create another.

VI. One must distinguish between [1] a physical cause, which works to achieve an effect through a natural impulse or its own form, and [2] a moral [cause], which, without such input and impulse of the will, by by way of an accomplishment contributes to an effect, like one who gives a ransom for the redemption of a captive is a cause of moral liberty, although he himself does not actively loose the bonds, and in this way perhaps a creature could contribute to creation, namely not by way of an instrument, but behaviorally as an agent.

Antithesis

I. Some scholastics hold that the power to create can be communicated to a mere creature as to a principal cause; e.g. Durand de Saint-Pourçain says that some creature can be produced, to which, as to a principal agent, it belongs, by native power, to create; Car. Franciscus d'Abra de Raconis says: "A creature can be the principal cause of some creatable entity." Avicenna says: "A creature can create something by way of a principal cause, undergirded by the general concurrence of God."

II. That a creature can be taken by God and used by God, through almighty power, as a supernatural physical instrument, to produce something out of nothing, is held by some scholastics, like [Peter] the Lombard, Thomas [Aquinas], Suárez, [and] Tanner, who hold that just as God gave the sacraments the causative power of grace, as to instruments of His power, so also could He communicate creative instrumental power to a creature. The rest of the scholastics, although, with Durand and [Peter] the Lombard, they do not clearly say that, yet they take an undecided stand regarding that problem and, in the usual way, speak to both sides of the matter.

III. Lalemandetius says that it is most probable that creative power can be divinely communicated to some creature. [Peter] the Lombard, Thomas [Aquinas], and Suárez are followed among others by Ebelius and Slevogius.

Confirmation

The thesis is proved [I] from Holy Scripture, which makes the work of creation proper to God alone in such a way, that it sets it [creation] apart especially, with a note, from false gods, Psa. 06:5; Isa. 45:5; Her. 10:11; the exclusive particle is also expressly added, excluding all beings outside of God from the work of creation, Job 9:8: Isa. 44:24, be they principal or instrumental causes.

II. From lines of thought drawn [1] from nature itself and the condition of creation, for which an infinite and independent force and power is required, at least in regard to nonbeing[1]; but this cannot be communicated to a creature, unless the whole divinity to be communicated. Therefore also the very action of infinite power, that is, creation, cannot be communicated. Just as God alone enjoys infinite power, so also can He alone remove the infinite distance that exists between Being and nothing. [2] From the contrast between Creator and creatures. Creatures cannot be creators, because they are and remain creatures. [3] From the unity of infinite power. Infinite power is not, nor can be, other than one but by such (namely digressive) communication it is multiplied and divided. [4] From the condition of creatures, who do not have infinite power and who can neither exist nor act independently. For they are either matter itself or an act totally composed of[2] matter and potentiality, and so they cannot act outside of matter. For the manner of existing in matter does not allow a manner of existing outside of matter. The angels themselves are also composed of potentiality and have a subjective mode of existing with regard to immanent acts. And so the act of no creature is equal to the production of something out of nothing. Briefly: The power to create is denied to a creature because it is a creature. (5) From the nature of an instrument. For (a) every instrument works dispositively and preparatively and through its own action in line with the purpose of the principal agent. But in creation no subject preexists, regarding which a creature can function as an instrument by its own previous action. Therefore no creature can be an instrument of creation or cooperate with God to crater anything. (b) In every instruments it is required that it have some particular power of its own, by which it of itself contributes something to produce the purpose of a superior agent, just as a saw, while it contributes to produce a bench, itself, by its own ability, cuts the wood, whereas otherwise an instrument is used in vain, if it is altogether idle and at rest. Now, a creature has nothing of itself, by which it could be joined with the creator's action and production out of nothing, and so it cannot contribute to creation, not even as an organ or instrumental cause.

III. We argue thus: "Whatever cannot be connaturally joined to the essence of a creature, but rather destroys it, cannot be attached to a creature. Now, the power to create cannot be connaturally joined to the essence of a creature, but rather destroys it. Ergo." The major [premise] is unquestioned. The minor is proved by this, that every creature, as regard its own whole being, depends on another. Therefore the power to act independently cannot be connaturally joined to its essence. "Now, since the power to act independently cannot be connaturally communicated to its nature and essence, the power to create also cannot be joined connaturally to its essence as a principal cause. Now, to the nature of no creature" etc. Ergo. The major [premise] is clear, because that power to create is the power to act independently not only [1] by a subject as it produces something out of no preexistent matter, but also [2] by a superior agent, because creation is the first of all acts, by which the being of the things shared[3] can be communicated; and that first act of all cannot originate except from a prime agent.

IV. From incongruity: If any creature could contribute in any way to creation, the argument drawn from the work of creation against the Jew, Arians, [and] Photinians, for building the deity of the Son and the Holy Spirit, would fall For if some creature could produce something out of nothing, not everyone [who] could be called creator would be God.

V. From the fathers, Irenaeus, Epiphanius, Athanasius, Cyril, Basil, [and] Augustine, who hold that, in proving the deity of Christ from the work of creation, no creature, even [one] in line with the absolute power of God, could be the principal cause of creation. Athanasius says: "To administer belongs to creatures and servants, but to make and create [belongs to] God alone and His Word and substance."

VI. From the scholastics and papists. The following teach that a creature cannot be a principal cause of creation nor be taken as an instrument for creating: Aegidius Romanus, Alexander of Hales, Bonaventura, Richard, [Duns] Scotus, Gregory of Valencia, Molina; these are followed by Fonseca, [Isaac de la] Peyrère Estius, Vázquez, and others.

Vindication

The opponents object: "It is indeed true and clear from plain passages of Scripture, that God created and creates whatever there is and is created of creatures, but it is not equally certain and just as evident from clear Scripture, that the power to create belongs to God in such a way, that it can in no way belong to a creature." Hence Gabriel Vázquez says: "I really do not see from Scripture how this view can be gathered. For the passages indicate only, that it belongs to God to have created all things. Now, there is nothing to prevent some creature from possibly coming into being that would be able to create something." Hence also Gabriel Biel says: "This conclusion, that no creature can create, cannot be proved." And Pedro Hurtado Mendoza says: "Hardly any convincing reason is advanced, by which it might be proved that a creature cannot create by its own nature." We reply: (1) Scripture expressly teaches, that infinite power and might are required for creation, which is production out of nothing, from nonbeing into being, Isa. 40:26; 42:5; etc. Now, it is clear that no creature has either infinite power or [infinite] being; it therefore follows, that no creature can create. (2) Scripture says not only that God created and creates all things, but also that there is no one besides God, who might create or produce something out of nothing. In fact, Scripture ascribes both creation itself and infinite power to create to the one [and] only true God in such a way, that it establishes therein a mark of distinction between false gods and the true and most high God.

Refutation of Objections

I. Lalemandetius objects: "One who can annihilate can also create; now, a creature actually annihilates." We reply: The major [premise] is denied. For less power[4] is required for something to be reduced from a state of perfection into an imperfect state, with which it was not in contradiction and [toward which it was] sometimes inclined, rather than that something be made out of nothing and brought into the state of being, for which it had no relation. And the minor proposition is simply not true. For the natural bodies that seem to be annihilated are really not reduced to nothing, but only broken down into their smallest parts.

II. They object: "A beatific creature, seeing the infinite God, forms a mental word representing God Himself, and so he makes something finite out of something infinite; now, it is not a greater implication, that a creature produces something out of nothing, than that he makes [something] finite out of [something] infinite." We reply: (1) It us asked that a creature makes [something] finite out of the infinite God as he forms a mental word from Him. (2) The line of thought is denied, for to make something out of nothing is of far greater power than to make a finite likeness of something infinite, representing to some extent that [infinite thing].

III. Observe: Restriction to a certain order of to a kind of things to be created and manner of chiefly acting, depending on the general concurrence of God, does not help [our] opponents, for (1) creation is nowhere restricted to this or that being, and although this restriction be granted, yet infinite power is still required, since there is all kinds of disrelation also between definite nothing and [definite] being. (2) It is absurd to fancy a cause of creation dependent on concurrence of another cause. For what depends on another in operating cannot be the cause of creation. For that production of something out of nothing, in which the nature of formal creation, properly so called, consists, excludes dependence of the creating thing in producing, not only from the subject, but also from the superior acting cause.

IV. Franciscus Bonae Spei argues: "Just as God, who gives being can also give working, so can one who gives being in such way, namely out of nothing of Himself and of the subject, also give working in such way, namely out of nothing both of the effect and of the subject. Ergo." We reply: the line of though is denied, because in the former, when God gave creatures being out of nothing of Himself and of the subject, He exercised His almighty power, but with regard to the latter, almighty power is not to be extended, so that He would give a mere creature the power to work out of nothing of the effect and of the subject, for this is impossible.

V. Observe: Most of the rest of the arguments that they advance beg the question when they assume that the power of creating is not infinite, that a creature can create dependently on a primary cause, [and] that the power of creating is compossible with the finite and dependent essence of a creature. Some also emphasized the omnipotence communicated to the human nature of Christ by virtue of the personal union, from which they hold that it further follows, that it does not involve a contradiction [to say that] a creature can create, at least by way of an instrument. But we have seen in the Exposition that the human nature of Christ is here not in controversy.

Notes:
1. *saltem ex parte Non-Entis.*
2. *actus immersus materiale et potentialitati.*
3. *esse participatum.*
4. *vitus.*

Question V

Were all things created out of nothing in the beginning?

Thesis

All things were created in the beginning not out of preexistent, or eternal, or previously created material, but out of purely negative nothing.

Exposition

I. Observe: The word "create," κτίζειν in Greek and ברא in Hebrew, taken (1) in the widest sense, means to produce something some manner or other, (2) less widely, [means] to make something extraordinary, new, and skillfully, Exo. 34:10: Num. 16:30, (3) strictly, [means] bring something forth, Psa. 104:30, (4) most strictly and properly, as well as in the usage of theologians, [means] to produce something out of nothing. So then, creation is an action by which a being is produced as regards its total self,[1] or, as the Thomists say, insofar as a being is, out of nothing, not as in a third or some other matter pertaining to its constitution, but as from a starting point, so that, just as there was nothing before as regards its total self now something comes into being as regards its total self. The circumstances of the text prove that in Gen.1:1 the word ברא implies properly the production of something out of nothing, and it is in other respects beyond doubt that the Holy Spirit spoke in the most proper sense in that passage.

II. One must distinguish between (1) the proper meaning of the word "create," where it is the same as to produce something allpowerfully and magnificently out of nothing, as in Gen. 1:1, (2) [a meaning] close to the proper [meaning], where it is, to make something out of crude and disordered matter, without previous disposition of the matter, like man was created, Gen. 1:27 and 2:7, likewise fish [and] beasts, [and] (3) a wide [meaning], where it is used of the performance of any and every kind of singular and stupendous work and miracle, as in Num. 16:30 [and] Psa. 51:10.

III. One must distinguish between [1] ἀρχὴν ἄναρχον, a beginning without a beginning, namely the Son of God Himself, who is called ἀρχὴ [beginning], Col. 1:18, α and ω [alpha and omega], Rev. 1:8, and ἀρχὴν ἔναρχον [beginning in beginning], or κατὰ χρόνον [with regard to time], beginning of time. Not the former, but the latter is meant in Gen. 1:1, as a comparison of the passages in Psa. 102:25; John 1:1, [and Heb. 1:10] clearly shows all of which also some of the ancients, Origin, Basil, Augustine, etc. hold.

IV. One must distinguish between [1] negative[2] nothing, which mean ἀφαίρεσιν [exclusion] and negation of every entity, or which denies every kind of being of the whole producible matter and so presupposes nothing either of the matter or the subject, but is not in conflict only with being, how the very first chaos was created out of nothing, that is, out of no preexisting or previously present material, and [2] private nothing, which is [so] called because of deprivation, or rather because of indisposition; it indeed presupposes matter, [which] however, [is] altogether crude, disordered, and unfit by its own nature, so that it is with good reason regarded as nothing. Here we do not mean privative nothing, but negative nothing.

V. One must distinguish between [1] the first and direct creation, or that, which is absolutely out of nothing, and this has no previously present matter, and [2] second, or indirect creation, which is out of thing in a relative sense, because it has previously present matter, but [which matter is] disordered, crude, and unable to produce the [intended] goal,[3] and in which alone is given compliant power, or ability not to be in conflict over against the prime cause, which acts with infinite power. All things were produced out of nothing, but some directly, like that crude and unarranged mass of heaven and earth, Gen. 1:1, and others indirectly, namely with the matter as means that God had previously created out of nothing, Gen. 1:20 [and] 24; 2:7 [and] 22.

VI. One must distinguish between [1] direct creation with regard to the efficient cause; this excludes every coefficient cause, both principal and instrumental, and so all things were created by God alone, and [2] direct [creation] with regard to the matter, because of which it is called direct creation, which excludes all preexistent matter; and the question here is about the latter.

VII. Observe: Some distinguish creation, with regard to the things produced, into κτίσιν, ποίησιν, and πλάσιν [creation, making, and molding], of which the first can be called production out of no matter, the second [can be called production] out of altogether crude [matter], and the third [can be called production] out of [matter] prepared in some way. Thus Spanheim: "(The words are those of blessed Varenius) Now, the Hebrews here distinguish those three words in this way, that ברא is 'create,' that is, produce, wither out of negative nothing, or out of privative [nothing], or out of previously existing matter of natural indisposition, to which κτίζειν [create] or the Greeks corresponds; עשה [make], put in order, embellish and finish the shape of a created thing, with the form composed, to which ποιεῖν [make] of the Greeks corresponds; יצר, or πλάζειν[4] [fashion] of the Greeks, denotes figuration and was used particularly for the marvelous figural [figuration] about to be made, as surpassingly and singularly used by the most holy Trinity in man, Gen. 2:7, and, in His own way, in the formation of the animal, or beasts of the earth, and the birds, [Gen. 2:] 19, and to this word יצר [fashion] is to be related the special word בנה [form], or He made, formed in a special sense, which is used [Gen.] 2:22 only of the woman formed out of a rib of the sleeping man and marvelously fashioned as by cells formed for the comfort of a fetus in the womb. The use of this observation all of Gen. 1, and especially [Gen.] 2:3–5, 7 etc.; 5:1–2. Thus he."

Antithesis

I. Of pagan philosophers, like the Stoics, as well as Anaxagoras, Pythagoras, Plato, etc., who hold that the world was produced out of eternal preexistent matter, and Democritus and Leucippus, [who hold that it was produced] by a fortuitous concurrence of atoms.

II. Of ancient heretics, whom Tertullian calls Materialists, like Marcion, Hermogenes, the Hermogenists, and the Hermianists, as well as the Manichaeans, Seleucians, etc., who papered over the error regarding eternal matter, out of which God afterwards made all things.

III Of the Aqueans, as Daneau calls them, who held that water was not created by God but was always coeternal with Him.

IV. Of the Socinians, who lean to the same heresy [as that] of the Materialists, like Smalcius. And just as Moskorzowski denies creation out of nothing and tries to refute the arguments advanced against matter coeternal with God, so he openly supports the heresy regarding the eternity of primary matter.

V. Of Konrad Vorst, who says: "Nowhere in the Holy Scriptures is it clearly written, that the world and all things that are in it were created out of nothing," and he denies that one must necessarily hold creation our of nothing.

VI. Of Episcopius the Arminian, who says: "Nowhere in Scripture is it said in [so many] words with or without controversy, that matter was made out of nothing.

Confirmation

The Thesis is proved [I] by the omission of mention of any material. Moses, deliberately about to set forth the account of the creation, makes no mention of matter, but simply says: "In the beginning God created the heaven and the earth."[5]

II. By the proper meaning of the word ברא, create, which implies production of something out of nothing. For most strictly and properly, as well as by usage of the theologians, ברא means to produce something out of nothing.

III. By the circumstances of the text. In Gen. 1:1 the word ברא demands this interpretation of the bringing forth of heaven and earth out of nothing, because of the nature and circumstances of the state of the subject. For in the beginning, when, by creation, creatures began to exist, the Creator alone existed and could exist; with Him alone existing, all things besides Him were nothing.

IV. By a holy paraphrase of creation, which is this, that God calls τὰ μὴ ὄντα, ὡς ὄντα, the things that are not, as though they were, Rom. 4:17; cf. 2 Mac. 7:28; τὰ βλεπόμενα, the things that are seen, μὴ ἐκ φαινομένων, not of things that appear, Heb. 11:3; here, in the words μὴ [not] and ἐκ [of], a transposition is made for the sake of euphony. The natural order is εἰς τὸ ἐκ μὴ φαινομένων τὰ βλεπόμενα γεγονέναι so that the things that are seen were made of the things that do not appear. And by τὰ μὴ φαινόμενα [the things that do not appear] are meant τὰ μὴ ὄντα [the things that are not]. Theophylact [says] on this passage: "Since God, by a word, created the things that are out of those that are not, what things does the line of though show us? None whatever, but faith alone." Therefore, that the world was created ἐκ τῶν μὴ φαινομένων [out of the things that do not appear] is the same as that the world was created out of nothing. Cf. Pro. 8:24.

V. By the line of thought: It is clear that the world was created by God. Therefore He created it either out of nothing or out of something; if out of something, the question arises in turn about that: is it created or uncreated: if created, the same question arises again: is it out of nothing, or rather out of something. Therefore there will be granted either an ongoing chain to infinity, or it will need to be said that the world was created out of nothing, or, finally, one must hold that it was created out of nothing, or, finally, one must hold that it was created out of matter coeternal with God; either this will be God Himself, or there will be two infinite and eternal principles, which [is] absurd.

VI. By the definition of creation, which is, according to Thomas [Aquinas], "the whole emanation or production of an entire entity made by God out of nonbeing, or nothing." Or, as he says, "the production of a thing with regard to its whole substance, with no previously posited matter."

Sources of Rebuttals

I. One must distinguish between the little term "out of," which is either [1] a mark of an efficient cause and denotes "of" or "from," as in Rom. 11:36, and it is not taken in that sense in this passage, for in that way the world would have been created by nothing, but would exist by chance or of itself. Or [2] it is a mark of matter out of which, as when Adam is said [to be] made of the dust of the ground, Gen. 2:7, but it is not taken in this sense here either, for it would follow, that the world would be created out of nonexistent and disembodied matter, since it is certain that there was nothing whatever beside God before the creation of the world. Or, finally [3], it is a sign or mark of point and order between [a] nothing, or nonentity, and [b] entity, and that in line with our way of understanding and speaking, by which we think of nothing itself as the starting point from which, so that it means the same as out of nothing preexisting.

II. Observe: "Nothing" is said either [1] of what is not, in such a way that being categorically conflicts with it and is called impossible, or [2] of what is not, yet in such a way that being does not conflict with it, and so is possible. In this passage not the former "nothing" but the latter is meant, and in this sense [Duns] Scotus said: "No thing is created of[6] nothing," that is, of the purely impossible, which in no way, with regard to understandable being, either possible or wanted,[7] could be in God, or in the divine mind, power, and will, and so Wycliffe said: "The power of God does not extend itself to nothing and a vacuum," that is, God cannot are that that is something, which involves a contradiction and that a vacuum as such is something.

III. One must distinguish between [1] the beginning point of creation, which [point] is overruled by creation, and [2] the end point of creation, which is brought on by it. The beginning point is nothing; the end point is something. For when it is said, "God made all things out of nothing," matter is not denoted, but the beginning point and the character of material cause is denied and order is denoted, so that just as it is said that midday comes into being out of the morning, that is, after the morning, so also does something come into being out of nothing, that is, something comes into being after nothing.

IV. Observe: Philosophy, teaching that nothing comes out of nothing, does not speak against this theological truth regarding the creation of the world out of nothing. Nor [does it say] that this is philosophically true, theologically false or contra. Because that action is true, [but] not without limitation, of the finite power of nature, which does not operate without the concurrence of matter, with the power of God always intact; although He does nothing contrary to the law of nature, which He Himself established, yet He could and still can do what He wants over and above that [law]. Or: That "nothing comes out of nothing" is true without exception, if by "comes" you mean "is generated," and the laws of natural generation do not bind the power of God.

Notes:

1. *secundum se totum.*
2. Pieper/Engelder: *wirkliches Nichts*/absolutely nothing.
3. *inidoneam ad termini productionem.*
4. = πλάσσειν.
5. The words are really God's.
6. *de.*
7. *volitum.*

Question VI

Were all things made together and in one instant?

Thesis

All things were not made in one moment or instant, but [were] created by God in a period of six days.

I. Observe: That all things were made in one moment indeed seems congruous with reason, but is contrary to Mosaic Scripture.

II. Observe: Creation can be thought of both ἀποφατικῶς, negatively, and καταφατικῶς, affirmatively. In the former way we do not need to think of creation as a kind of a way of generation, or ἀπορροῆς [emanation], or of emanation out of the essence of God, or of successive motion, or of some laborious undertaking, or also natural change (for God made all things by a word). In the latter way we must think of it [creation] partly as an instantaneous production, party as both a wise [1] arrangement and [2] equipment of things that would be produced, Psa. 33:9, 104:24; Jer. 10:12.

III. One must distinguish between the works of creation considered [1] in general and [2] in particular. In general, the work of creation is the world taken collectively, or in the aggregate, with its parts, both visible and invisible, both substantial, which can properly be called created, and accidental, which [can properly be called] concreated. And in particular, the works of creation can be distinguished according to their order of production presented by Moses. According as the various ones began to be produced in six days [of creation], Eco. 20:11.

IV. One must distinguish between [1] divine power, which, as it is infinite, could thus have created the whole world in a moment, and [2] a second act or work of divine power, which [work], since it is determined by the free will, wisdom, and goodness of God, is therefore also not to be judged or assessed apart from omnipotence, and so that successive production of things is not to be ascribed to a defect of divine power, but to the will and wisdom of God, and it does not imply a kind of decrease of powers, but praise of order.

Antithesis

I. Of some of the fathers, like Origen, Athanasius, Augustine, [and] Procopius of Gaza, who hold that the world was created by God in a moment and that the six days are to be taken allegorically. Arnold Carnotensis tries to prove "in one day" and "creation made" from Gen. 2:1.

II. Of Philo the Jew, Cajetan, and especially [Jean] Bodin. Who say that those days pertain more to distinguishing the order of things than to true intervals. R. Moses the Egyptian also clearly teaches momentaneous creation of all things. R. Nachamani says that the whole universe was made on the first day and was brought into the clear[1] on the following days. Blessed Affelmann says: "We are not impressed if someone objects that it is of unsophisticated simplicity to hold that the world was fashioned in the course and space of six days, by that the whole of it was created in one point of time, but Moses, in relating the work of [creating] the world, uses the division of six days for the sake of teaching, namely because of the dullness as well as the simplicity of the Jews for whom he wrote. It is also the view that somewhere has [as] follower blessed Augustine and Thomas [Aquinas], who leans the same way, and some [who are] more recent." Thus he. In short: The view that all things were made in one instant was concocted by rabbis, encrusted by Cajetan Melchior Canus, newly supported by Nicolaus Abraumus, a Jesuit, and embellished with new paradoxes; for he holds that the substance of all things, except the soul of man, was produced together in the first moment of time, and that in six days, by natural emanation, all things came forth according to their natures,[2] and moved[3] by natural inclination to [their] natural place. Blessed Calov refuted this view.

Confirmation

The Thesis is proved (I) but he account of creation, set forth in Gen. 1, in which [account] all the words are to be understood historically and properly;

and one is not to depart from the clear statement, unless the analogy of faith, what precedes and follows, and other circumstances call for this; now in that [account] Moses (ὁ ὑδογενὴς [the one drawn from the water], or born in the water,[4] in fact drawn from the waters of origin,[5] on command of the sterile daughter of the Pharaos, as Josephus says) says in the clearest words what was made by God on each day.

II. By the sanctification of the Sabbath, for which matter this reason is given in Gen. 2:3; Exo. 13:6; and 20:11: because, just as He [God] created the world in six days and rested on the seventh, so He wanted also the Jews to work on six days in each week. This reason would carry no weight, says Rivet, if God had created all things in one moment, and not successively through more days. "Against that bold view of Augustine and the allegorical view flowing out of it" (says blessed Varenius) "(1) the clear division of creation into six days; (2) the limitation of that creation on the sixth day by the specificative ה [article], as well as by the added universal כל-אשר עשה [all that He had made], Gen. 1:31, and by ויכלו [they were finished], Gen. 2:1, and by the express term, "the seventh day," Gen. 2:2, taken exclusively; (3) the obligation of the law regarding the Sabbath both with respect to God and which respect to sanctifying the day. For if God solemnly instituted this Sabbath day for this reason, that on it He finally ceased from the work of creation as finished, then He did not cease on the individual days τοῦ ἑξαημέρου [of the hexaemeron], but created; [4] also the relation of the pronoun אלה [these] in this v.4 of [Gen.] 2 to the account in [Gen.] 1."

III. By the line of thought: If all things were made at the same time, some reason would need to be given for the order of that Mosaic account. For in setting forth the distinction of six days, Moses observes either the order of nature, or the order of rank, or the order of knowledge, or the order of time. Not the order of nature, which creatures have among themselves, for in that way he would first have needed to tell of the creation of the firmament, then of the stars, then of light, and then finally go on to plants and offshoots and various other things that needed to be told of. Not the order of the rank of created things; in that way the creation of man would have preceded; it followed later, in last place. And not the order of knowledge, whether you regard God or man. There remains, then, that Moses followed the order of times, in which some things were made earlier, others later. Some observe that, in creating visible things this order was followed by God that the sequence would be, Gen. 1, from the more imperfect to the more perfect things, and first, that those that have only being were created, v. 9; then those that [have] also quickening [life], v. 11; third, those that [have] also intellectual [life], v. 20; finally man, bestowed in addition with a rational soul.

Sources of Rebuttals

I. One must distinguish between [1] a sense of the account of creation written by Moses that is literal, proper to the Holy Spirit, and intended by Him, and [2] its allegorical and figurative interpretation; because of the uncertain allegories dreamed up by human imagination, one should not depart from the letter in the sacred accounts and in the articles of faith.

II. One must distinguish between [1] actual production, which began with the first beginning of time and ended with the complete finish of the six days, and [2] the potential production of the same [six days], which took place on the first day with matter, to which that potential was given. According to Thomas [Aquinas], Moses, in Gen. 2:4, speaks not of the former, but of the latter. Or: when Moses says, "On the day on which the Lord God made the heaven and the earth," one wrongly gathers, from the singular יוֹם [day], the production of all things in a moment, because by יוֹם [day] is meant the whole period of time of creation, and thus that ἑξαήμερον [six-day period], or certainly the last four day period, which was עֲשׂוֹת יוֹם [(the) day He made]. And He [God] says יוֹם [day] in the singular number, in order to indicate that His singular work was done on individual days, and that this arrangement of heaven and earth was made in order.

III. One must distinguish between a day [that is] (1) definite and distinct from the second and the third [day], (2) "day" used collectively for "days," and (4) taken distributively. In Gen. 2:4 the word "day" can be taken either in the second or the third or the fourth way, and so, taken in the last way, one can repeat, on the basis of what precedes: On the day on which God made the heaven and the earth, and on the day on which He made the virgultum[6] of the field and every herb etc.; or, in the third way, the word "day" is to be taken collectively for the time of the six-day period.

IV. One must distinguish between [1] a συλλογὴν [sylloge[7]], totality, and equality of condition of the works of God, how all creatures in general, with none excepted, were created by God, John 1:3, and [2] συγκαιρίαν [simultaneity], coincidence in time, or momentaneous creation, which was performed without all succession of time. The words of Ecclus.[8] 18:1 are to be taken not of the latter, but of the former: "He that lives forever created all things κοινῇ [jointly] together." For the Greek word κοινῇ [in common] is to be explained [as] jointly, simultaneously, by a common law, unitedly, etc., and so it does not denote identity of time, but togetherness of condition; and it is not to be taken χρονικῶς [chronologically] but συναγωγικῶς [collectively]. It likewise denotes [1] togetherness or origin and dependence, or [2] continuation of noninterrupted time, because all things were created within that one six-day period, or also by reason of their matrix, so that once could say that all things were made at the same time in that primeval chaos. Gregory seems to have that in mind [when he says]: "God created all things at the same time, materially, but not formally, by the substance of the matter, but not by the kind of the form." Hottinger says that it is a fallacy of composition and division. For the word "together" or "jointly" does not pertain to "He created," but to "all things," that is to say, God created all things together in such a way, that nothing more was created later, and that nothing can be taken away from that creation.

V. Observe: In Job 40:15, by the word "behemoth" ("Behold now behemoth, which I made *tecum* [with you]") by virtue of the plural number, either beasts in general, or elephant, or other kinds of beast that are like plurals are meant, which [were] created on the same day with man; and so other take τὸ [the] "with you" in a comparative way for "just as also you" in the first creation and [on] the same day; others explain [it] as *apud te* [by you]: "Whom I made *tecum* [with you], that is, *apud te* [by you] on earth, not in the waters, like leviathan. If Satan is meant by "behemoth," that "I made with you" can be explained, that he was created together with man, and that both are words or that he was made like man, and that both are works of God, or that he was made like man, having a mind and free will, and that he was also at the beginning made good and right, or that he was made with man within the same six-day period. But it is more correctly said that the word "behemoth" is attached to the devil only in an allegorical sense and with some accommodation.

Notes:

1. *in apertum.*
2. *qualitates.*
3. *contenderint.*
4. *Aquigena.*
5. *natalibus.*
6. twig, shoot, or sprout.
7. compendium; collection.
8. Ecclesiasticus; Sirach.

Question VII

Was a primitive and unarranged mass made in the beginning, which provided the matter of the heavenly and elementary bodies?

Thesis

On the first day a primitive and unwarranted mass, or that confused chaos, was made directly out of nothing; out of it afterwards, on the following days, the world, and the things that are in it, was produced by divine power.

Exposition

Observe I: The question here is, what is meant in Gen. 1:1 by השכים [the heaven] and האלצ [the earth]? [Does it mean] the totality of created things, and so all the things that the whole first chapter [of Genesis] specifically mentions, David repeats in Psa. 104, and St. Paul briefly summarizes in Col. 1:16, so that this is a kind of general summary of the whole chapter, in which way Gen. 1:1 does not pertain only to the account of creation on the first day, but would also be πρότασις [an initial statement] or proposition of the whole chapter and a summary of the account of creation? Or does "heaven and earth" rather mean that primitive and unarranged mass, out of which the creatures then emerged by the word of God?

Observe II: The first view seemed not improper to blessed Chemnitz. Pareus, Grotius, and others have also embraced it. But if that first verse is a summary of the whole chapter and account of creation, (1) it would be required that that תהו ובהו [without form and void], as well as that תהום [deep], the unarranged, primitive, unformed chaos, which the waters enveloped and fermented, that abyss of amazing ἀσχημοσύνης [want of form], either existed already before the creation, or Moses did not set forth the creation of those things. [And] it would follow, that that prime matter either [1] clearly is uncreated, as the materialists hold, or, [2] as Episcopius would [have it], [it would have been] created before some times or ages preceding the six-day period of the creation. In fact, if those words briefly set forth the whole universe, [then] the creation of either heaven or earth would nowhere be related, because later only the separation of the waters is set forth, but not the creation of the heaven and the earth. (2) The word ברא [He created] would [1] not be taken in the meaning of creation whose starting point is negative nothing, for the object of that creation is nothing but the angels and that primitive mass, out of which all heavenly and earthly things were made, but [2] would be taken in the meaning of creation whose starting point is privative nothing, of [nothing] or privation and of natural indisposition, and so that absurdity again emerges, that heaven and earth were produced out of matter [that was either] [1] uncreated or [2] made before some times. (3) Nor does the word בראשית [in the beginning] agree well with that statement. For either [1] since that, of which it is the beginning, was a creature of the six days, the βαττολογία [tautology] would follow: "In the beginning of the whole creation God created the whole creation," or [2] the error of those who hold that the creation was made in a moment and a mathematical point [of time].

Observe III: We therefore hold with Lyra and blessed Luther, that by the name of heaven and earth, Gen. 1:1, is meant the primitive and unordered mass, that mass, confused and not yet set in order, which is called by the name of heaven and earth by a kind of πρόληψιν [prolepsis], with regard to the end point, conclusion, and purpose, because God produced that primitive mass to this end, that He might afterwards form heaven and earth from it. Some call this primitive and unformed mass chaos, some [call it] prime matter, yet for the most part different from the Aristotelian primitive matter (which occurs more correctly only abstractly in a concept of the mind, than outside the mind in the truth of the matter).

Observe IV: Moses means this ethereal and arial heaven and the earth in the precise respect (as Varenius says) of material lack of form, primitive condition, and amazing ἀσχημοσύνης [want of form], or in respect of the prime mass and unformed but, and so those words stand here in accidental substitution, for, you see, only later, on the second day, did the expanse receive the name *Schamaim*[1] [heaven], and only on the third [day] did the dry [land] receive the name ארץ [earth].

Observe V: The author of the Book of Wisdom, 11:17, calls that primitive mass mad on the first day ὕλην ἄμορφον [formless matter], not because it was devoid of all form, but because it was primitive, unformed, lacking that full and final form, which it received on the following days. And in the same way it is called a primitive, unformed, and unwarranted body, because, by reason of its substance, it was partly earth, partly water and mud. (Zanchi calls the water muddy and the earth water), by reason of size, a mass huge and, as it were, without foundation, [and] by reason of [its] nature, primitive, unformed, dark, and ἀόρατον [obscure], as the Hebrew is translated by the Septuagint [Gen. 1:2].

Antithesis

I. Of some papists, like Peyrère. Here are also to be classified all those who by the heavens made on the first day understand the empyreal heaven. [More] on these later.

II. Of some Calvinists who deny that a primitive and unwarranted mass was made in the beginning, like Keckermann, who write: "What some hold, that God made all things out of some kind of primitive and unwarranted mass, which poets have called chaos—that has no basis in the canonical Scriptures and conflicts with divine perfection." [Also] Piscator, Tilenus, and Francis Gomar, [who says]: "Moses indicates that 'the heaven and the earth,' Gen. 1:1, does not mean 'the primitive and confused chaos' of the world, and the 'prime matter' of celestial and terrestrial things (as many hold), but 'heaven itself and earth itself,' since he clearly says, with the demonstrative article and, as it were, a pointing finger: השמים הארץ, this heaven, this earth, which are already seen." Also Gisbert Voet. Lambert Daneau is also usually cited in favor of this view, but he clearly says that for him the more probable interpretation and view is that of those who would have heaven and earth (as mentioned in Gen. 1:1) indeed created by God out of nothing in the beginning, but as the primitive matter of the whole future work and [orderly] world, out of which God, by His power and might, produced the rest of the things.

Confirmation

The Thesis is proved (I) by the connection of the text and by the explanation of Moses himself. For Moses immediately adds in v. 2: והארץ "and that same earth," namely, of which he had spoken in v. 1, was תוהו ובהו, "void and empty." The Chaldean translates: "And the earth was desolate and empty to [the point of] amazement."[2] The Septuagint: ἡ δὲ γῆ ἦν ἀόρατος καὶ ἀκατασκεύατος, "the earth was obscure [and] unformed," not yet fashioned, that is, primitive and unarranged. For these words, "Tohu" [without form] and "Bohu" [void], in the Scriptures usually imply amazing vastness and disorder, as is clear from Isa. 34:11 [and] Jer. 4:23. "From this it is clear," says Daneau, "that there was a kind of a primitive mass of a future world, a seedbed and matter, prepared by God Himself only then, and not from eternity. And it cannot be denied that there was also something of disorder then in the heaven itself, since the celestial and terrestrial materials were not yet set apart and separated from each other, which was done later and on the second day. For no [part] of heaven was as yet adorned, and no brightness or light show in it. And that confusion was even greater on earth. Therefore it was described as 'Tohu' [without form] and 'Bohu' [void]." Thus he.

II. By the designation "deep" [KJV]. For Moses adds: "And darkness was upon the face תהום of the deep,' that ask that primitive and unordered mass, which the waters covered and fermented, lacked all light within and without. Now, the word תהום [deep], contradistinct from the earth of that primitive and unordered mass in this passage means the unformed and deepest water, which covered and enveloped that while goose of the earth everywhere, as in a deluge. For not until the second day did God produce the firmament, or heaven by distinguishing and separating it from the waters, and not until the third day, with the earth separated from the water, did dry land appear and the waters recede into the deep, gathered from the terrestrial globe; this separation necessarily presupposes σύμμιξιν [intermingling] and mixture, that is, chaos of heaven earth, and waters thoroughly mixed, as blessed Gerhard teaches.

III. By David's account in Psa. 104:5–6: "Who fixed the earth upon its foundation; it will not be moved forever and ever. The deep like a garment [is] its vestment. The waters stood above the mountains. At Your rebuke they fled; at the sound of Your thunder they were afraid." These words tell of the divine work of the first day (1) that at that time the earth was fixed, which on the third day, with the waters gathered into one place, was made very dry, but not founded or made, cf. Job 38:6. (2) That the deep was the garment of the earth. For that disordered chaos was enveloped and covered by the multitude of waters, as with a ragged and dark garment; these [waters], at God's rebuke and the sound of [His] command ("Let the waters that are under the heaven be gathered into one place," Gen. 1:9), went in a big rush to their places. By this rebuke that unwarranted disorder of things was corrected, as David says; [and] as blessed Polykarp Leyser puts it: "God saw the disarrayed chaos and the disorder of the earth and the water in which all things undulated as [in] muddy mire. That displeased Him. Therefore He said, speaking more severely to the waters; 'Be gathered into one place, so that dry land may appear.' There you would have seen the marvelous speed of the waters, how one part rushed into the hidden depths of the earth, [and] the other part stood as if gathered together into a leather bag; they vied with each other in obeying God, who commanded.³"

IV. By the view of the Jewish church. That this [church] held that view namely that in the beginning the primitive and unformed matter and mass was made, can be gathered from the Book of Wisdom

11:18: "For You omnipotent hand was not impotent; it also created the world ἐξ ἀμόρφου ὕλης, out of matter without form" [v. 17 in the LXX]. They therefore believed that in the beginning the unformed matter, that primitive and unwarranted mass, [was] made without [its] completed form; out of it, in turn, the other things were created by virtue of the omnipotence of God.

V. By the consensus of the better commentators, both ancient and more recent. Justin Martyr speaks of this view as well known and unquestioned by the common people and shows from this, that Plato took his [view] first from the church. He says: " Plato most certainly received [it] from our learned teachers, because he said that God, with the unformed matter changed, created the world (ὕλην ἄμορφον οὖσαν στρέψαντα τόν θεὸν κόσμον ποιῆσαι). Hear the very words of Moses, the first prophet, as drawn up also by all the older Greek writers, through whom [Moses] the prophetic Spirit, telling how and from what God made the world, begins thus: 'In the beginning God made the heaven and the earth. And the earth was obscure and [was] unordered" etc. Basil the Great indicates the same, saying: "The heaven, which was made in the beginning, was made like the earth was made, lacking order and unadorned, and was later beautified with light the sun, [and] the moon." Augustine says: "Heaven and earth are here called prime matter, because out of it on the second day heaven and on the third day the earth was to be made." The same is apparently intended by those who say with Gregory the Great: "The substance of things was indeed created all together, but the form was not shaped at the same time; and what appeared through the substance of the matter did not appear at the same time through the form of the shape." Eucherius [says]: "Matter was made from nothing, but the form of the world [was made from] the unformed matter, which was called by the name of heaven and earth not because this already was, but because this could be." Of the more recent [commentators], the following agree with Luther's view set forth above, which is also our [view]: Gesner, Runge, Lyser, Pelargus, Gerhard, Affelmann, Varenius, and others, and of the Reformed: Zanchi, Polanus, [Peter] Martyr and Junius; [also] Daneau [and] Alting.

Refutation of Objections

I. Peyrère, Keckermann, Gomar, and Voet: "In the Hebrew it is emphatically said: 'God created השפיח והארצ,' with the *hajediah*, notificative or demonstrative ה [article], that heaven, which we now see, and that earth, on which we now stand." We reply: The prefix ה is sometimes also taken in an indefinite sense, as in Deu. 8:3 [and] Lev. 18:5, and even if, at the very most, it is granted that here it means a specific and definite thing, or τὸ δὲ τὶ [that of which], this heaven, this earth, yet it does not follow, that at that time heaven and earth were already established in their complete and perfect being, for the added account of Moses does not allow it. Augustine says:

"That matter is called heaven and earth not because it already was this, but because it was able to be this."

II. They object: "That improper interpretation of the words 'heaven' and 'earth' for chaos and the original matter of the world cannot be proved by any use of Scripture." We reply: We agree that the Scriptures cannot mean that elsewhere, since they speak of heaven and earth as they now are; but here the Scriptures explain how they were in the beginning before the separation was made. It suffices, therefore, that here they are described in this way, that they were "without form and void."

III. They object: "In that way, nowhere and never in the six-day period is mention made of the creation of heaven and earth, if it is not state in v. 1." We reply: It certainly is mentioned, not only inasmuch as they were created indistinctly on the first day in that original and unwarranted mass, but also inasmuch as the heaven was distinctly made out of it on the second [day], and the earth on the third [day].

IV. They object that in that way the creation of heaven and earth out of noting is excluded. For if heaven and earth were created out of chaos as the original matter, [they were] therefor not [created] out of nothing, that is, out of no matter. We reply: Even if the other things [were] created out of that original matter, yet that mass was created directly out of nothing; again, the primeval light and the angels, the soul of Adam, [and] the other things [were] created indirectly.

V. In Wis. 11:21 it is said: "God created all things by number, weight, and measure," that is, very distinctively and in the most well-ordered way; if so, He created no confused chaos. We reply: Wisdom speaks about the absolute works of creation, insofar as they are in being, and not about works to be completed, inasmuch as [they are] still in [the process of] becoming; such work was the original mass.

VI. They object: "God is the Author of order, not of confusion: it conflicts (1) with the nature of the Creator, in the beginning to gather things among themselves and mingle [them] in one mass, and later separate and form the things to be created out of that mass; it conflicts also (2) with the nature of creation, which [is] the prime, noblest, and most well-ordered act of God." We reply: (1) These arguments are opposed to the very text of Moses, in which it is clearly stated that the earth was vastness and emptiness, full of darkness and thoroughly mingled with waters and finally separated from them on the third day. (2) God is not therefore the Author of confusion because confused chaos was first created; but He showed Himself the Author of order by that very fact, as Alting confesses, since order, in line with the nature of the Creator here comes into being, as is shown also by the preservation of species through new individual propagation, for, you see, a tree does not come into being complete, all at once, but first it is a sprout, nor is a human fetus complete all at once, but first it is a κύημα [the initial matter conceived], then an embryo, and finally an infant. (3) Creation is not to be called confused, but only an original, unwarranted, and incomplete work of creation. And because the act of creation is completely well ordered, therefore there is an ongoing chain in it from rudiments to completion. (4) And this is not to be connected with the power of God, what it was possible for Him, as almighty, to do, but with His will and wisdom, what it pleased His wisdom to do and how [it pleased His wisdom] to do [it].

Notes:
1. Transliteration of the Hebrew word for heaven(s).
2. *ad stuporem.*
3. *utraque alteram obedienta Creatorem praecipientem antevertere voluerit.*
4. *intelligatis.*
5. Transliteration of a Hebrew term that means demonstrative article.

Question VIII

Are there waters above the firmament of heaven?

The Point at Issue

The question is not (I) about clouds, but about waters true and properly [so] called; not about their special use and why they are, but about [their] general use and purpose and whether they are.

Thesis

There are supercelestial waters encircling heaven everywhere. For in the primeval creation God put true and natural waters, completely homogenous with the subcelestial, or lower [waters], above the heavens decked out with heavenly bodies on the fourth day as Holy Scripture says.

Exposition

I. One must distinguish between the book of Scripture and [the book] of nature. We do not perceive the super celestial waters by sense, nor do we know them by reason, but we understand from Scripture alone both why and what they are.

II. One must distinguish between [1] waters true and properly so called and [2] allegorical and imaginary waters. "The better parts of theologians always understood waters properly [so] called, which, they hold, God, in a wonderful and marvelous way, truly and really put above the firmament, or starry heaven," says blessed Meisner.

III. Observe: The supercelestial water is not defined by element, because it is not programmed for the production or creation of mixtures, but, as Sperling explains, it is a "simple natural body, completely encircling heaven, curved out of the original division of the waters to the glory of God and the completeness of the universe." The body is natural, because [it is] of the same kind as the subcelestial [water]. It is called simple, because of the simple matter of water. The accidental difference is drawn partly from the place that was assigned above heaven, partly from the origin, namely the first division of the waters, partly, finally, from [their] purpose. And we know only the final and universal, not the special or particular purpose, which is to praise God, as is clear from Psa. 98:4 and the Song of the Three Children in Daniel, as also to complete the universe. For God and nature do nothing in vain.

IV. One must distinguish between [1] waters properly [so] called and [2] clouds which are properly not water, not in the higher regions of the air, much less above the air, but put in its middle region, nor finally do they come into being by division of waters (which is mentioned Gen. 1:6), but by resolution.

Not to say that clouds are a mid-air phenomenon; yet at that time, when the supercelestial waters were formed, there were as yet no mid-air phenomena, because these come into being simply thanks to the stars, which were made later, on the fourth day.

V. One must distinguish between [1] nature and [2] place, function, and purpose. The nature and essence of the superior and inferior water remains the same, although the former received a different place, a different function, [and] a different purpose by divine arrangement.

VI. One must distinguish between [1] division and [2] destruction of waters; division did not destroy the waters, nor did it take away their nature, but only separated and set apart with regard to places, so that some was raised above the heavens, [and] some [was] placed below the heavens. Place does not take away natures.

VII. One must distinguish between [1] τὸ [the] ὅτι [fact] of supercelestial waters both by reason of existence and by reason of use, and [2] τὸ [the] πῶς καὶ διότι [how and why], which is not known by us.

Antithesis

I. Or Origen, who by the superior waters understood the good angels, and by the inferior [waters understood] the evil angels, cast down out of heaven into this turbulent and dark air. Gregory of Nyssa suggests that by the superior waters the intelligible virtues are meant although he does not grant that by the inferior [waters] the devils are meant. Scaliger does not differ much from him, since to him [Scaliger] the superior waters are supercelestial hierarchies.

II. Of Augustine, who calls the superior waters spiritual [and] the inferior [waters] physical; but he retracted this view.

III. Of the scholastics, like Bonventura, Durand, Lyra, Tostatus, Cajetan, Catharinus, [and Peter the] Lombard, who by the supercelestial waters understand a new heaven, which they call crystal, aqueous, or glacial, or hardened like ice and crystal.

IV. Of the papists, like Peyrere, Gregory of Valencia, Bolduci, [and] Petavius, who by superior waters understand clouds and rainy waters, separated by air from the sea and discrete from streams.

V. Of most of the Calvinists, like Calvin, Keckermann, Mercier, Piscator, Zanchi, Polanus, Junius, Daneau, Timplerus, Drusius, Alsted, Sixtinus Amama, Voet, and Cloppenburg, who [plural] indeed understood waters properly [so] called, yet not raised above the heaven of the stars, but hanging in the clouds, Pareus calls it a falsification of the Jews that waters are above the firmament, and Calvin nothing better.

VI. Of some of those of our own country, like Dr. Georg Calixtus [and] Dr. Musäus, who by the supernal waters understand clouds or also waters in the clouds. Dr. Jacob Martini leaves the matter undecided because it is not sufficiently well known.

Confirmation

That there are supercelestial waters, and that they are of the same essence as the lower [waters], is proved (I) by the completely clear statement of the Mosaic text in Gen. 1:6-7: "[God] divided the waters that were under the firmament from those that were above the firmament." For mention here (1) is of the firmament, or more correctly expanse. For the word רקיע is properly "expanse," which God called "heaven," in which He later, on the fourth day, put large luminaries and the stars, [Gen. 1]:14. But the large luminaries and all the stars are set not in the air, but in the arched vault of heaven, the is, in the ethereal heaven. Therefore the ethereal heaven is to be understood by the name "expanse." (2) Mention is made of waters put above it [the ethereal heaven], which are called מים, waters, just like the lower [waters]; hence we understand that [the superior waters] are of the same nature and essence as those [lower waters], inasmuch as they [the superior waters] were at first joined together with them [the lower waters], later separated, and truly put above the expanse. Here one must also note that the word מעל cannot here be translated in any other way than "above" (the firmament).

If someone objects, that here we have not the little word על [above], but מעל [from above], [and that] מעל [from above] in such a connection means not over or above, but from above or from on top, *Von oben herab* (down from above), so that the meaning is "down from the expanse above," and so there is more reference to a concave than a convex heaven, and it means that those waters come down to us from a place higher than the expanse—rabbi Solomon Jarchi[6] would have it so, that מעל is used not without reason, because it denotes not only above, but also from above—it is nevertheless well known that the word מעל is the same as "over" or "above," as in Gen. 7:17 and 22:9. It is therefore translated ἐπάνω [LXX; above], and the contrast here is clear between the waters מתחת, under, and מעל, above, which [contrast] allows no other meaning than that. Therefore רקיע [firmament] was the divider that God set between the lower and the superior waters, and that division of waters was nothing else than the separation of the entire whole into its parts, so that the nature of the waters remained intact in each part. "Now, who would not believe the dividing Creator of nature regarding nature?," asks Bartholinus. "To divide water into two parts is not to make a cloud," says Sperling, "but to divide the entire whole into two parts of its nature and kind. Hence, as those waters [were] before joined [into] one [water] and had the same nature, so also separated, they retain that same nature and essence. For to separate and divide waters is not to destroy them." [Our] opponents object: "רקיע [firmament] does not mean only the ethereal or starry heaven, but also the air, or aerial heaven, for it is said clearly that the heavenly bodies were set in that heaven, which [heavenly bodies] were certainly not set in the air or in the aerial heaven, but in the ethereal [heaven]. Schindler, Hottinger, Jakob

Martini, Varenius, [and] others indeed would have the ethereal heaven and the air equally denoted, but the view of most of the fathers and of blessed Luther seems preferable, [namely] that only the ethereal heaven is designated here by the word רקיע, because in the account of creation it is not sufficiently congruent for both heaven itself and the air to be designated by one and the same word, and it is said in the verse quoted: "Let there be lights in the expanse of those heavens."(3) In v. 20 they also understand the ethereal heaven, but they explain it thus: עַל־פְּנֵ רקיע, from the region of or over against the expanse,[7] as Helvicus [says], or before the face of and before the presence of the expanse of heaven, or under the starry heaven. P[aul] Fagius says: "The preposition עַל, before, is also often taken as near [and] nearby, and the meaning is "under heaven in the air," or "near," that is, "next to" heaven. (4) That the air is called רקיע indicates also the air, but it remains to be proved that the word is applied to the expanse itself. (5) The air was not yet on the second day, but emerged later, when the waters were separated from the dry land on the third day. They object further: "מים [waters] denotes not only waters, but also clouds." We reply: Clouds cannot be understood by waters set above the celestial expanse. For clouds are properly not waters and are nowhere in the Scriptures called waters. See No. IV in the Exposition. Clouds do not come into being by division of waters properly so called, but by resolution of effluxes into aqueous droplets. In fact, as is clear from Gen. 2:5, clouds did not exist in that hexaemeron, since He [God] decreed those first days of the world to have been without clouds and clear, as Bonfrère says. And what, then, would be that division between the waters of the clouds and the lower waters that comes into being through the air? The air properly does not divide the waters, since it poses no separation, so that the [waters that] are above be not joined with the lower [waters]. We also argue thus: Whatever is set below the firmament is not called water above the firmament or expanse by Moses. Now, the clouds are set below the firmament. Ergo.

II. By the agreement of parallel passages: Psa. 104:3. In the sources we read: "Who builds His high, or upper places on the waters, making the clouds His chariot, walking on the wings of the wind." Luther: "*Du wölbest es oben mit Wasse* [You arch it above with water]." And Psa. 148:4: "Praise Him, heaven of heavens and waters above heaven."

Note: (1) In these passages neither clouds nor the air can be understood by waters, because neither one is properly water, [and] neither one is located above heaven. (2) David distinguishes the choir of celestial musicians that praise God from the choir of elementary and terrestrial [musicians], and he joins the waters above heaven to the former choir. Calov adds the Song of the Three Children: "'Waters that [are] above heaven, bless the Lord, ὕδατα πάντα τὰ ὑπεράνω τοῦ οὐρανοῦ.' In this passage," He says, "again in the series of creatures those waters are listed after the angels, but they are put before the sun and the moon and the stars and terrestrial [things], and therefore they cannot be understood otherwise than of waters above heaven. And although that song is ἀπόκρυφον [apocryphal], yet it shows regarding the faith of the Jews, that the ancients, namely the Jews, believed the waters [to be] supercelestial." Thus he.

III. By the ὁμοφωνία [agreement] of venerable antiquity, like Justin Martyr (who says that the back sides of heaven were weighed down with the waters and that the waters were laid upon the back of heaven), Basil, Chrysostom, Ambrose, Theodoret, Procopius, Augustine, Gennadius; likewise Bede and [John of] Damascus. Especially to be noted are the words of Luther; he says: "I indeed would have readily thought[8] that the firmament is the highest body of all, and that the waters hanging and flying not above, but under the heavens are the clouds that we see, so that in this way the waters divided from waters mean the clouds divided from our waters on earth. But Moses says in so many words that there are waters above and below the firmament. Therefore I take reason captive here and agree with the Word, even though I do not understand it. Most of those on our side today agree with blessed Luther, but in such a way that they confess with Augustine, that they do not know how and what kind of water are there. [Peter the] Lombard says: "But howsoever the waters are there, we do not doubt that they are there." Of the papists, [the following] admits supercelestial waters; Mendoza, Menochio, Molina, Becanus, [and] Bonfrère. Of the Jews: Phil, Josephus, [and] R[abbi] Onkelos in [his] Targum.

Sources of Rebuttals

I. One must distinguish between [1] the essence of the supercelestial waters, according to which they are altogether homogenous with the sub celestial or lower [waters], and [2] their qualities, namely lightness, delicateness, transparency, and incorruptibility, in which they are said by some to differ from the terrestrial [waters]. We say that the supercelestial waters have weight, yet they do not, as a result, descend, because they are not in a turbulent,[9] but a natural place, or one assigned to them by God, and they cannot descend, because they are not in a turbulent, but a natural place, or one assigned to them by God, and they cannot descend, because of the interposed expanse.

II. One must distinguish between [1] what is visible and [2] what is seen by the very act [of seeing]. It may be in this way, that the purpose of Moses was, to describe only visible creatures, in whose number, however, are also the supercelestial waters, although they are not seen by the very act [of seeing] because of the immense distance and what has been put in between.

III. One must distinguish between [1] a natural place, which arises out of the condition of nature and comes into being in a physical way and by a [physical] impulse, and [2] a supernatural [place], which comes into being in a ὑπερφθσικῷ [hyperphysical] way and depends solely on the power and will of the Creator.

The Calvinists object: "Above heaven there is no natural place of water." Bonaventura replies: That is natural, which and to which God made assignment in the first creation. Bede says: "He that fixes the waters retained below heaven for a time by the vapors of clouds, can suspend the waters above the sphere of heaven not by vapory tenuity, but by glacial solidity, so that they do not fall; He also suspends the mass of the earth in nothing. [Regardless of] how that waters are there, it is unquestionable that they are there."

IV. The Calvinists object further: "That water would be perishable." We reply: There is no danger of perishability. For what would cause it? Solar rays are not projected above the firmament of heaven. And why cannot God keep those waters from corruption? He that commanded the water to be divided by an interposed and middle ground firmament provided how the divided [waters] might also remain separate. Ambrose says: "The word of God is the power of nature and the substance of durability, as long as He wants it to remain, who ordained [it]."

V. One must distinguish between [1] the general use and purpose of the supercelestial waters, which is the amplification of divine power, wisdom, goodness, and majesty, Psa. 148:4, and [2] [their] special purpose and use, which escapes us; yet the matter itself is for that reason—that its special purpose is unknown—not to be denied, because [to argue] from our ignorance to denial of the matter does not follow. We rather acknowledge with Augustine: "The authority of this Scripture is greater than the capacity of our intellect." We say that the uses that [John] of Damascus mentions namely cooling the heat of the stars and shielding against the impact of the winds of heaven, are thought up without basis. The Jewish comment of Josephus and Philo is about cooling the heat of the heavens and the stars or about compressing the heavens, lest they be shaken by the turbulent violence and storms of winds.

VI. Observe: No one on our side denies that "heaven' is often taken for "air"; but is it proved that it is taken that way in this passage? Hence the things differ greatly that are said to occur in heaven, from heaven, out of heaven, and the things that are said to be place above heaven; this having been said, all examples drawn from parallel passages in support of an opposing view fail.

VII. Observe: The clouds (1) did not yet exist on the second day, (2) they are not waters, properly speaking, (3) they are not of the same nature as the lower waters, (4) they are not in a higher place, namely the highest region of the air, [and] (5) they are not always the same. When the proponents of the opposite view say that they understand the waters of the clouds, not the clouds, and that the clouds are subjectively or materially waters, the question arises: Where were those water when the subject was not yet created? In that hexaemeron the clouds did not yet exist.

Question IX

Was the heaven that they call empyrean, which provides a palace for God and a dwelling place for the angels and saints, created before all things?

The Point at Issue

The question is not (I) about the physical, starry, and visible heaven, but about the heaven that they call empyrean, or resplendent. (II) The question is not whether it is a certain πού [somewhere] of the saints, distinct from the πού [somewhere] of the damned, but whether it is a certain, physical, and definite place created by God and appointed for the angels and saints.

Thesis

An empyrean or resplendent heaven, which most scholastics and other papists, also the Calvinists, hold [was] produced on the first day and in the first instant of creation and placed above the firmament for a dwelling place of the angels and saints and even God's own palace, is a sweet dream without sleep and a pure figment of the aforementioned heterodox people; both Scripture and nature say nothing of it, and it neither existed nor will ever be.

Exposition

I. Observe: Although the heaven of the saints is not a physical place, yet it is not therefore nowhere, but somewhere; or, it is not everywhere, nor nowhere, but somewhere. But precisely where it is, is not easy to say.

II. One must distinguish between [1] the physical, starry, and visible heaven, of which Genesis and the physicists speak, and [2] the heaven that they call empyrean, or resplendent, which provides a palace for God and a dwelling place for the angels and saints, and that was created on the first day; the question here is not about the former, but about the latter.

III. One must distinguish between [1] the ethereal, or starry, heaven, in which the luminaries and stars are set, and [2] the aerial [heaven], in which the clouds are and the birds fly. The name "heaven" is applied not only to the ethereal, but often also to the aerial region, as in Gen. 7:11; 8:12; Deu. 4:19; Isa. 55:10.

IV. One must distinguish between (1) a specific, physical, and definite place created by God and appointed for the saints and angels; such a heaven neither is nor will be; (2) a ποῦ, or somewhere, of the saints, distinct from the ποῦ [somewhere] of the damned, in which the souls of the pious are gathered after release from the body and are made partakers of heavenly blessings, [with] which we also agree, in which the souls of the pious are gathered after release from the body and are made partakers of heaven blessings, [with] which we also agree, but in such a way, that we hold that in this darkness of nature we can penetrate neither its essence, nor nature, nor location; and finally (3) the stare of the saints, or their everlasting blessedness and heavily glory, which is neither creator nor creature, but rather the happiness of a creature resulting from or born out of the clear and intuitive[1] vision of the Creator.

V. One must distinguish between [1] the heaven of God and [2] the heaven of the angels. Although God manifests Himself in the heavens in a special and glorious way to the angels and saints and presents [Himself] to be enjoyed and to be seen; yet one may not assign to God some created dwelling place set above these visible heaven or hold the heaven of God and the angel for one and the same. For the "where" of the angels is defined, but the majestic heaven of God can be circumscribed by no limits, and it is nothing else than the eternal and infinite glory and majesty of God, which God had in Himself from eternity and will have to eternity, and the divine, heavenly, omnipresent, and omnipotent rule over all things; see 1 Kin. 8:27 and 39; Psa. 2:4, 45:7; 103:19; 113:5; Isa. 44:14; 66:1.

VI. One must distinguish between (1) the heaven of nature, which is either aerial or ethereal, (2) the heaven of grace, which is the church on this earth, Mat. 20:1, and (3) the heaven of glory, which is that most holy and most blessed heaven, in which God manifests His glory to 2 Cor. 12:2, says that he was caught up.

Antithesis

I. Of most of the scholastics and papists, who laboriously argue and speak agreeably about the heaven of the saints, which they call empyrean, and its location and qualities, as well as the exercises of the saints in that fictitious heaven, sometimes indulging in purely carnal and mundane speculations. And most hold that this heaven is located under the sign of the creation of the world. Becanus ventures to write that this heaven has a very solid foundation in Scripture. "For," he says, "Scripture teaches that the firmament and all things were made[2] on the second and fourth day." He adds: "The firmament is in the middle of the waters in such a way, that some waters are above [and] some [are] below the firmament. If that is so, it follows that the heaven that was created in the beginning is above the firmament and above all waters, which truly can be nothing else that empyreal. Spondanus depicts the empyreal heaven like this, that it is a heavenly body, the most elevated and [most] magnificent of all that are in the whole world, indeed that is completely[3] distended over all the heavens known by philosophers and astrologers and is therefore, because of excellence, in the Holy Scriptures called heaven of heaven and heavens of heavens. And it differs also from the others, because, whereas they are in a continuous circular motion, it remains unmoved, so that as a result, no lack of theologians has not hesitated to say that it is not spherical, like the rest, but has a square form.

II. Of the Calvinists, who hold that the heaven of the saints is a physical place, created above this corruptible world and above all heavens, and that it has space and distinct local places, in which one may move, sit, stand, walk, etc. Thus Hieronymus Zanchi says: "The heaven of the saints, angels, and human beings, set above all visible heavens, created by God, is of physical substance, incorruptible, extremely large, [and] perfectly brilliant." The following agree: Walaeus, Ames, Alting, and Joh. Cloppenburg, [who] says: "The first work of the first days is that outermost and highest heaven, the third heaven, the heaven of heavens, which [is] physical and therefore local, and in which," he says, "is the seat of God and the throne of God." [Also] Joh. Bergius [and] Spanheim, [who] says that there is that heaven, with regard to substance very obscure,[4] with regard to quantity very large and a true place, with regard to quality very bright, with regard to duration forever in [its] essential nature,[5] [and] with regard to location way above and exalted over all visible heaven. The *Admonitio Neostadiensium*[6] (which, in the judgment of Massonius, has a place among the public writings of the Reformed) assigns a local dwelling place to God in common with the saints, angels, and blessed. But they differ among themselves in some things, for some would have the heaven of the blessed be of physical substance, but others say that it is indeed a place, and on high as to local situation, and created, but leave it undecided whether it is physical, e.g.,

Gregarious Francus, a theologian at Frankfort [on the Oder], and the rest of the theologians at Frankfort on the Oder, as the above-mentioned Francus says, who speak at considerable length about the heaven of the blessed. Timpler makes that heaven devoid of matter and form, though he regards it as physical. Bullinger, on John 14:2, goes along with the scholastics so far as to hold distinct small cells and mansions, a place, a seat, and a promenade in the heavens; the following fancy the same: [Peter] Martyr, Ursinus, and Martini. But the rest, though they hold that it is a created and physical place, yet they do not venture to specify anything certain regarding its qualities. Most, finally, hold that the heaven of the blessed is the same as the heaven of God, but some seem to deny that.

III. Of the Socinians, who restrict God to a certain place and hold that He is not present in His substance except in heaven, which for them is the place of immortality, the dwelling place of God, situated above the starry expansion.

IV. Of the Arminians, whose leader, Episcopius, would have the heaven created in the beginning be as a suitable dwelling place in which the angels would be gathered and which God wanted to be His palace.

Confirmation

The error of the opposite view and the truth of our [view] is proved (I.) by [this] line of thought: If it is such an empyreal heaven as is imagined and deceived by the scholastics and Calvinists, then it can be perceived either [1] by sense of [2] by the mind, and this either by reasoning and understanding or by faith. But it can be perceived in none of these ways. Not by sense, because according to [our] opponents, it is invisible and intangible, and not by reasoning, because we know it neither [1] deductively, or by a line of thought, nor [2] inductively, or by effects, since it cannot be grasped by a line of thought, nor does any effect touch us. Nor, finally, is it perceived by faith, since Scripture sets forth clearly neither sets essence, nor [its] quality, nor [its] location.

II. By the denial of accurate knowledge, Isa. 64:4; 1 Cor. 2:9: "Eye has not seen, nor ear heard" etc. Now, if the heaven of the blessed were such a place as is described by the scholastics and Calvinists, it would certainly either impact the senses or enter the heart of man.

III. By the silence of Scripture. Scripture says that, with respect to us, the heaven of the blessed is on high (in words that indicate a place, describing sublimity of state and condition), but that some space [the was] created on the first day is physical as to substance, very large as to size, and a true place, very bright as to quality, forever in [its] essential nature as to duration, way above and exalted above all visible heavens, or embracing the starry heavens all around and on all sides everywhere,[7] Scripture nowhere indicates that, and therefore it is rash to want to define it in that way. "Because it is not for us in our frailty to investigate the mysteries of the heavens," as Augustine says. Hence also Bonaventura points out that it is better, regarding this matter, piously to doubt than rashly to define anything.

IV. By Mat. 18:10, where the angels are said to be on earth and guard little children and at the same time to be in heaven and see the face of God the Father διὰ παντὸς [always]; hence we conclude irrefutably, that the heaven of the blessed or of the angels is not a created place, very remote from the earth and set above the starry heaven, because in that case the angels cannot be in heaven while they are on earth. And so the angels, who by reason of place are not absent from the earth, are by reason of state and condition also at the same time in heaven. That continuity of appearance before the Father in heaven does not rule out presence and διακονίαν [ministration] among the saints and little children on earth. Therefore that "where" of the angels can be in heaven, and this heaven of the angels can be on earth with little children, and so the angels are never outside heaven and outside the contemplation of God (which is the very heaven or blessedness of the angels), not even when they minister to saints on earth.

V. By the conflagration of the visible heavens on the last day, 2 Pet. 3:7 and 10; Psa. 102:26; then either the heaven of the blessed will also perish, since it lies next to the starry heaven, according to the new of [our] opponents, or it will have to escape from that πανωλετρία [complete destruction], and this escape will have to be shown from Scripture.

VI. Observe: That the heaven of the blessed is a certain ποῦ [where] distinct from the ποῦ [where] of the damned is gathered from Luke 16:26, where a great gulf is said to be fixed between the bosom of Abraham and hell. Now, just as hell denotes a certain [ποῦ] [where] of the damned, so the bosom of Abraham denotes the ποῦ [where] of the blessed, without determination of place.

VII. The heaven of the blessed and of the angels must be something different from the heavens created by God at the beginning of the world. For these will finally pass away, Luke 21:33 ("Heaven and earth will pass away"). But that is eternal, 2 Cor. 5:1; Heb. 12:27. And how would the heaven of the blessed be called new, which God will still create, Isa. 65:17; 66:22; 2 Pet. 3:13; Rev. 21:1, if it was made at the beginning of creation?

VIII. Observe: That the heaven of God is distinct from the heaven of the angels is proved by Mat. 21:25 and Luke 20:4, where the baptism of John is said to be from heaven, not of men, that is, from God, for men are set in contrast to God, not to heaven, Luke 15:18: "Father, I have sinned against heaven," that is, against divine majesty. For one certainly does not sin against the heaven of the angels or against any creature, but only against God, Psa. 51:4; Dan. 4:26: "Your kingdom will be firmly established after you will have acknowledged that the heavens rule," that is, that the divine majesty [rules]. For the heaven of the angels does not rule. Therefore the heaven of God is not the heaven of the angels, but divine majesty and power itself. Thus also the Son of Man, being on earth, is in heaven, endowed with heavenly majesty, although not disposed in its full use,[8] John 3:13; heaven, whence the Holy Spirit was sent, 1 Pet. 1:12: from where God properly looks, Psa. 14:2: 33:13; where he hears our prayers, 1 Kin. 8:32; Psa. 18:6. And this heaven is God Himself.

IX. Dionysius Petavius [says it] best: "As to that heaven, way above all, and not falling below the one that is seen, in no way can it be denied to be a blessed and heavenly dwelling place above all, assigned to the [good] angels and all saints, but of what kind it is, is not said, except in conjectures and human comments. Thomas [Aquinas] says of this heaven that it consists in no other way than in line with the view of Strabo and Bede, as well as of Basil; but many more mention it, however they do not call it empyreal; that is a useless and foreign word. For it is also not called ὁ ἐμπύρεος, so that it would be fiery, but ἔμπυρος [brilliant]."

Refutation of Objections

I. One must distinguish between [1] higher and lower things with regard to place and situation and [2] higher and lower things with regard to glory and dignity as well as ignominy and misery. When the heaven of the blessed is called higher and the ποῦ [where] of the damned [is called] lower, [this] speaks not of place and situation, but of state and condition, namely of dignity and ignominy. The former denotes supreme happiness, the latter [denotes] supreme misery.

II. Observe: When the heaven of the blessed is described by the words house, tabernacle, Paradise, dwelling place, city, etc., then descriptions of that kind are to be understood not σωματικῶς [physically], but μεταφορικῶς [metaphorically] and μυστικῶς [mystically], because it is a house ἀχειροποίητος [not made with hands], 2 Cor. 5:1, a spiritual Paradise, etc. and future happiness is described in the words of this world.

III. Observe: When Scripture ascribes a seat, a throne, [or] a dwelling place to God, then it speaks ἀνθρωποπαθῶς [anthropopathically], but it must be understood θεοπρεπῶς [in a way worthy of God], according to the [statement] of [Gregory of] Nazianzus: "πολλὰ ἀνθρωποπαθῶς λέγονται, ἀλλὰ θεωπρεπῶς νεοῦνται. Many things are said humanly, but they are to be understood divinely"; namely so that divine majesty and power are devoted. So also when it [Scripture] says: "The Lord is on high; He dwells on high," Psa. 93:4; 113:5 Mark 11:10; Luke 2:14, that is to be explained not τοπικῶς [locally], of some high place, but τροπικῶς [figuratively] of the eminence of the majesty.

IV. Observe: The kingdom is said to be prepared for the blessed ἀπὸ καταβολῆς κόσμου [from the foundation of the world], Mat. 25:34, not by reason of outward creation and production, but by reason of eternal decree and constitution. It is also said that it was to be prepared by Christ, John 14:2, namely because the glory and happiness, prepared for the godly from eternity by God by destination, is prepared by Christ through satisfaction, merit, and conferral.

V. Observe: When we are told to seek and to set our mind on the things that are above, Col. 3:1, the point is not the elevation of places, but the fleeing of earthy lusts and embracing the heavenly and sublime life: in fact, Christ is not more above by reason of places than below, because He is exalted to the right hand of God, which cannot be defined by spaces of locations. "Set your mind," says the apostle, "τὰ ἄνω [on the things above], μὴ τὰ ἐπὶ τῆς γῆς [not on things on the earth]." Here those little words, "ἄνω [above]" and ἐπὶ τῆς γῆς [on the earth]," are not to be taken τοπικῶς καὶ σωματικῶς [locally and physically], so that a place above or below is designated, but καινῶς, in a new way, a spiritual and heavenly [way], namely so that τὰ ἄνω [the things that are above] mean the things that are pleasing to God, holy, [and] just, [and] those that are on earth denote sinful and evil things, as Paul says in [Col. 3,] v. 5.

VI. Observe: If all things that are said about the heaven of the blessed were to be taken κατὰ ῥητὸν [literally], it is necessary that we envision there not only mansions, but also tables, places at tables, and feasts—the kind of a Jewish and Muhammadan heaven that we readily lead to [our] opponents. Meantime we wonder why they, especially the Calvinists, want to maintain τὸ ῥητὸν [the literal sense] throughout, which they, however, plainly do not want to allow in other mysteries, especially [that] of the Holy Supper.

VII. One must distinguish between [1] ποῦ, a real, or extrinsic "where," that is, one that are diverse and distinct from the body itself, and [2] an imaginary ποῦ [where], which is not distinct from the body itself, but [is] intrinsic to [the body] itself and that the mind so conceives. So also can the blessed be in God alone without a place, or an external physical "where," and so not in a real but an imaginary ποῦ [where].

VIII. Observe: The heaven of the blessed, or of glory, is called the third heaven in 2 Cor. 12:2, not [1] by reason of place, or διατακτικῶς [by order of arrangement], as the Calvinists would have it, as though the lowest heaven is aerial, the middle [heaven is] ethereal, [and] that highest [heaven] of Paul, [is] the third, or [that] of the blessed, but [2] by reason of number, or διακριτικῶς [by way of distinction], so that it is distinguished from the first two heavens, namely the heaven of nature and the heaven of grace, and that to them [the blessed] is assigned not a place, but a sublimer dignity.

IX. One must distinguish between [1] a seat and [2] the state of the blessed. A seat is in a certain ποῦ [where]. For the blessed are categorically not nowhere, but certainly somewhere; however, we cannot with certainty define where they are. "Their spirits return to God," Etc. 12:7. "They are in Abraham's bosom," Luke 16:22; "in the hand of God," Wis. 3:1. Doubtless neither God, nor the hand of God, nor Abraham's bosom is a created place, but the state of the blessed is wherever God manifests Himself and His glory to them, Mat. 17:2; 18:10.

X. Observe: Dannhauer well says: "That audacity is to be rebuked, which defines (the heaven of the blessed) as a situation depicted by Bullinger and set forth [by him as] a location above the visible heavens and called permanence. For where do the brazen little people get this? When Christ ascended, He covered those more sublime things with a cloud as with a veil"; cf. 1 Cor. 2:9. "This view is wrong; reason is lacking."

XI. The same Dannhauer says: "The arguments of the papists are pure sophistry, moving from genus to species: Given[9] a heaven above the firmament; Paul was caught up to the third heaven, say the highest heaven; blessedness demands a most excellent and most brilliant place; therefore these is given an empyreal heaven in the picture that is formed in the scholastic brain. What if the heaven of the first day would not differ from the heaven of the second day as to substance, but only as to form, order, and glory? What if the third heaven, to which Paul was caught up, were incorporeal? What if the heavens of heavens were the immeasurable ἀπρόσιτον [unapproachable] heaven of God? What if the glorious bodies were illocal?"

XII. Observe: If you translate הַשָּׁמַיִם [with] "heaven," like the Vulgate in Gen. 1:1, or "heavens," as the Vulgate translates [it] in Gen. 2:1, it is the same, for it is only duality, like מִים [water; waters], which in meaning is unaffected by the singular and the plural number. But out of that consideration of duality the empyreal heaven is wrongly fabricated, of which there is deep silence in Moses, and the conjecture of the Jesuits is plainly uncertain: In Gen. 1:1 the Vulgate translates the word *Schamaim*[10] with "heaven" and in Gen. 2:1 with "heavens"; therefore in the former it meant only the empyreal heaven,

[and] the latter both the empyreal [heaven] and the firmament, or ethereal [heaven]. Those who in [Gen.] 1:1 understand only an empyreal [heaven], [and] in Gen. 2:1 principally [understand] the same with an ethereal heaven, must in Gen. 1 in the word "earth' conceive of an ethereal earth. So this would be the interpretation: In the beginning God created an empyreal heaven (the seat of the angels) and the earth (i.e, a body, which, after separation, [was] divided into the elements and orbs of the heavens, the lower part of which is called earth), which is very silly.

Notes:

1. or direct.
2. *producta.*
3. *latissime.*
4. *subtilissimum.*
5. *indefectibile ab intrinseco.*
6. Written by Ursinus against the Formula of Concord, at Neustadt, in the name of the Reformed, who had established a base of operations there.
7. *undiquaque.*
8. *non in plenario eius usu constitutus.*
9. *datur.*
10. Transliteration of the Hebrew word for "heaven."